The Mother-of-the-Bride Book

ALSO BY SHARON NAYLOR

The Groom's Guide

It's My Wedding Too

It's Not My Wedding (But I'm in Charge)

Mother of the Groom

The Ultimate Wedding Registry Workbook

What's Your Bridal Style

The Mother-of-the-Bride Book

Giving Your Daughter a Wonderful Wedding

Sharon Naylor

Citadel Press
Kensington Publishing Corp.
www.kensingtonbooks.com

CITADEL PRESS BOOKS are published by

Kensington Publishing Corp.
119 West 40th Street
New York, NY 10018

All Kensington titles, imprints, and distributed lines are available at special quantity discounts for bulk purchases for sales promotions, premiums, fund-raising, educational, or institutional use. Special book excerpts or customized printings can also be created to fit specific needs. For details, write or phone the office of the Kensington special sales manager: Kensington Publishing Corp., 119 West 40th Street, New York, NY 10018, attn: Special Sales Department; phone 1-800-221-2647.

CITADEL PRESS and the Citadel logo are Reg. U.S. Pat. & TM Off.

First trade paperback printing (updated edition): May 2015

10 9 8 7 6 5 4 3 2 1

Printed in the United States of America

Library of Congress Control Number: 99-28530

ISBN-13: 978-0-8065-3765-8
ISBN-10: 0-8065-3765-5

First electronic edition: May 2015

ISBN-13: 978-0-8065-3766-5
ISBN-10: 0-8065-3766-3

To

Rose Foglio Montenaro Potuto

and

Joanne Blahitka

Contents

Acknowledgments

THE AUTHOR would like to thank the following people for their invaluable assistance with this book.

My agents Elizabeth Frost Knappman and Ed Knappman, for tirelessly finding good homes for my work, supporting me through the writing process, and cheering me on.

My editor Andrew Richter, who braved the dangerous highways to get to meetings with me, recommended excellent additions to the book, and always called with good news.

Laura Shmidt and Tara Bruno, for quickly and efficiently researching and delivering their material.

All of the many wedding vendors who contributed their advice and demonstrated once again why they are the best in their business: Steve Blahitka of Back East Productions, Rich Penrose of Dean Michaels Studios, Angela Lanzafame of The Potted Geranium, and all of the others.

To my parents, for helping me plan just about every special event in my life.

To my grandmother Rose, for the whispered inspirations.

And to Irene Blahitka, who lives on in art and memories.

A Note to the Mother of the Bride

Congratulations! Your little girl is getting married!

This is the beginning of a very special time in your life. As you help to prepare for your daughter's wedding day, your entire life will be caught up in the swirl of activity, the excitement, the creative process, the celebration. As mother of the bride, you'll be the second busiest woman in the bridal scene at your house. All at once, you get to plan, coordinate, and contribute—and watch your daughter transform into a glowing, radiant bride.

Can it be that she's all grown up now and ready to go off into a life of her own? Can it be that she's now the bride when it doesn't seem so long ago that she was a little girl playing dress-up in your closet or climbing the trees out back? She will be a beautiful bride, and you will be every bit as beautiful and radiant as mother of the bride.

This is a magical time, Mom. Cherish every moment.

A Note From Your Daughter, the Bride

_____

_____

_____

_____

_____

_____

_____

_____

_____

_____

_____

Part One

Wedding Planning Essentials

1

Your Role as Mother of the Bride

ONCE THE INITIAL EXCITEMENT of the announcement wears off, you'll start to realize that Mother of the Bride is not just a title. It's an actual role with a list of responsibilities and dos and don'ts. There's much more to it than just looking lovely in a pale pink dress in the first row at the ceremony.

So just what's involved in the new title that's been bestowed upon you? What exactly is your role as mother of the bride? Unfortunately, it's not always as clear-cut as that of the bride or the groom. The details of the position vary widely from wedding to wedding: some mothers run the show, from making financial decisions to choosing colors to drawing up the bulk of the guest list. Some hand over a blank check and show up smiling on the wedding day. Some just show up smiling on the wedding day.

Clearly, a major break has occurred in recent times from the traditional role of the mother of the bride. Bridal guidebooks from past decades list the jobs that were to be taken on by the mother of the bride. If you look at a 1950s guidebook, the list is tremendously long. Today's bridal guidebooks and bridal magazines offer the following list, always with the caveat that the selections are purely optional. The list is merely a jumping-off point, with individual duties to be discussed by the bride and her mom.

Traditional Responsibilities of the Mother of the Bride

- Help plan the details of the ceremony and reception
- Assist in choosing the bridal gown and trousseau
- Help choose the wedding vendors—caterers, photographers, florists, and so forth
- Help choose the guest list and design the seating chart
- Record wedding gifts
- Record invitation responses
- Choose her own wedding wardrobe
- Communicate with the mother of the groom on complementary wedding wardrobe
- Communicate with the father of the bride on the details of the wedding
- Communicate with the groom's family on the details of the wedding
- Serve as official hostess at the reception
- Offer support and guidance to the bride

This, believe it or not, is not the 1950s list. Variations of it appear in every wedding magazine as today's standard. However, no bride wants to be bound by this list, as if it dictated hard-and-fast rules to live by. The bride may choose to handle recording her gifts or selecting caterers on her own. The list, then, should not be viewed as a "See, it says it right here. This is my job" contract. The bride will not agree, and you'll only foster resentment. The list is merely a guide to consult with the bride so that decisions can be made about your role on an individual basis.

Customs have changed since the time when you were married and have certainly changed even more since the old days before your time. If you think about who, historically, has been in control of weddings, you'll see that in Western society, control over a marriage was initially in the hands of the father. In ancient and medieval times, the daughter would be virtually "sold off" to a suitable man. Deals were made, perhaps some cattle was exchanged. In those days, marriage was a matter of survival. Families were formed to create a cooperative entity, in which the man hunted or farmed, and the woman managed the home and cared for the children. Entire communities had a role in choosing and arranging marriage partners. As time went on, and as we as a people progressed and advanced, couples began to choose one another, and the marriage was formed with the help—not the ultimate control—of the family.

If you look back to movies of the 1950s and 1960s, weddings were a big deal, and the parents' role in the marriage was emphasized. Think about the original version of *Father of the Bride.* (That's the Spencer Tracy/Elizabeth Taylor version, not the Steve Martin remake.) While the father stressed the details of the wedding, it was the mother who supported the bride and helped her make her decisions. There, too, the family's help was noted.

In the 1970s, we had weddings on our favorite soap operas and sitcoms. The mother of the bride was portrayed as a sack of nerves, often caricatured as a runaway mom with a garish clothing ensemble. This poking of fun, once it shows up on television, is a commentary on the times. In that decade, the mother of the bride maintained her role as keeper of the family and all things domestic, and the daughter's wedding fell under her particular domain.

In the 1980s, money flowed. Now, more than ever, weddings became lavish affairs, and with all that extra cash, the mother and father of the bride could afford to give their daughter a far better wedding than they had had themselves. It was a decade of decadence, and in many ways people were measured by the toys they had; the creation of a drop-dead gorgeous wedding was more a statement of the parents' position than of the bride's and groom's wishes.

In the 1990s, the mother and father of the bride have fallen even further behind in the category of control. Now, more than ever, men and women have equal status in the working world, and they are perhaps far more independent in their own rights before marriage. They wait longer after college to tie the knot, and their own self-sufficiency undercuts the parental control that existed in previous decades.

As time went on, the parents' control has faded in most situations. Traditions of old, which used to prescribe that the bride's family would pay for—and thus control most of—the wedding, are just as often the exception as the rule nowadays. Not all Moms and Dads shell out big bucks for the big day, as more and more couples opt to pay for their own weddings. In some cases, depending upon the financial status of both families and the couple, and depending upon mutually agreed-on arrangements, the groom's family covers all costs. Basically, anything goes.

Your role, then, may be completely traditional or else totally unique. And you may be powerless to influence which way it goes. The bride and groom hold all the cards, and you will have to wait to see which category they choose.

Whatever your level of involvement and control, you're still the mother of the bride. You're still your daughter's confidante and cheerleader, support system, and cold-feet warmer. In many ways, yours is considered the backbone role of the wedding. A wedding is an emotional time for everyone involved, but for the bride it is also a time of adjustment. Her entire life is about to change, and she senses that. If she has been living self-sufficiently, the idea of sharing a home with the man she loves may be frightening. Or it may be her first time living on her own—a double adjustment. If she has lived with her fiancé before marriage, perhaps simply the change in her title to that of "wife" can be overwhelming. To her, the image of "wife" may have been formed by pictures she's seen in movies and on television. More than one bride has had a panic attack about someday winding up in a fuzzy bathrobe and curlers, yelling at her husband about the toilet seat being left up. The words *ball and chain,* tossed around in jest by relatives, will hit a nerve with her. She has probably just become familiar with who she is after childhood, college, and her entry into the real world, and now she faces a new leap into another dimension. These issues prey upon her mind, and she needs you to assure her that she can handle whatever comes. She also needs you to assure her that she has what it takes to make her marriage work, and that she can—and should—remain in her old identity even as part of a married couple. She needs you to assuage her fears so that she can enjoy this process.

You are not only preparing a wedding, you are preparing your daughter for this big change in her life.

"What about the change in MY life?" Yes, your daughter getting married means that your life, too, will change, and it is important for you to realize several things. First, forget about wailing, "My baby is going away!" She hasn't been a baby, much less your baby, for a long time. Granted, seeing your daughter in a wedding gown brings back memories of her playing dress-up bride at six years old, and you long for the days when she was small and, let's face it, completely dependent on you. But she's a grown woman now, and if you haven't adjusted to that yet, it's time to start. You also have a new son-in-law coming into the picture. Your daughter loves him, so no matter how you feel about him, if you haven't yet accepted him as one of your own, it's time to do that now—for your daughter's sake.

Your daughter getting married doesn't mean you're getting older. You would be the same age today if your daughter remained single. Her life change doesn't catapult you into senior-citizen status. Too many mothers look at their daughters' weddings as a tearing-away, a pronouncement of ending. It is not. It is, rather, a new beginning for her, and for you. It is an opportunity for you to allow her to assume a new role and learn all kinds of new things that you have learned over the years. Your best approach, then, is not to hold her back from this wonderful new adventure. She will sense your uneasiness, and that will only compound her fears. The best thing you can do is show her how genuinely happy you are for her, lead by your example, and assure her that she should enjoy this time.

You've raised a wonderful, intelligent daughter who is strong enough to handle this transition, no matter how frightened she is to look over the cliff's edge at this big leap. As the mother bird, you know she must leave the nest, so it is your job to give her a supportive nudge, smile, and watch her take flight.

And so the stage is set for the big sand trap that faces all mothers of brides: I know I'm supposed to be there for support—that, I get—but just how much involvement and control do I have in the details? How much can I do without stepping on toes? Where does my role begin and end in the *fun* stuff?

Among circles of brides and soon-to-be-brides, the biggest horror stories revolve around the Runaway Mother of the Bride. She's the mom who took over virtually all aspects of the planning, who threw guilt trips like showers of rice, who tearfully cried, when confronted by a stressed-out bride and groom, "It's *my* wedding, too!" She may seem like a cartoon to you now, as you are not deeply mired in the sticky web of etiquette and great aunts who'd take offense at *that* song played at the reception. Just remind yourself every now and then—for your sake and the bride's— not to turn into the Runaway Mother of the Bride. Or your daughter may bitterly talk about you like this someday:

❧

My mom not only changed the colors of the reception decorations, she did it because they would clash with HER dress.

—Melanie, bride

❧

I wasn't allowed to invite any of my college friends or coworkers. All I heard from my mother was "I'm paying for it, so we invite my friends."

—Jenna, bride

❧

If I didn't have as much pride as I do, I'd drag the woman onto a talk show.

—Traci, bride

❧

My out-of-control mom ruined my whole wedding. I wish I could do it all over again.

—Anne, bride

❧

Think about these brides' quotes before you clash with your daughter over something as simple as the lettering on the cocktail napkins. Flip back to these pages every now and then and think about how you want your daughter to feel during the planning of her wedding, during the wedding itself, and for years afterward.

Remember, ultimately, you're there to assist, not to take over—*even if you are paying for the wedding.* You're there to see your little girl become a bride. You're there to nod your teary-eyed approval when she tries on that perfect gown. You're there to take the burden off her when she does need you to take over a few small tasks. Perhaps she's still in school and is in the depths of studying for finals. She'll need you to finalize some orders for her wedding, just weeks away. She'll need you to do the roundup work, to help her out and lighten the load a little. And then she'll also need you to hand the reins back to her when she's ready for them.

She'll need you to respect her wishes, to be diplomatic when you really want to scream, and to put up with all the stops and starts without driving her crazy about them, too.

Mostly, your daughter needs you to be there.

❧

It's nice just to be able to participate in the decisions, when asked. The ultimate decisions are the bride's and groom's, but I'm here to support them, whatever they choose

—Anna, mother of the bride

❧

What I appreciated most was that Mom was a good listener. Even when she didn't agree, she kept it in her mind that it was our big day, and that we were just trying to work out what we wanted. She was there for us completely, and I'll always remember that.

—Jen, bride

❧

2

Working With Others

CONSIDER YOURSELF THE GOODWILL AMBASSADOR of the wedding party. During the planning of every little detail, you'll find yourself dealing with many, many people—from the groom's family to the bridal party to the professionals who will cater, take pictures, and so on. A great part of your job is to coordinate these people, to light fires under them, if need be. If this sounds like "grunt work," so be it. Your daughter has a million details to worry about, so you'll help her tremendously by keeping the waters flowing.

Communicating With the Bride

We'll start by working with the bride, since that's the major part of your role. You're there to consult with, to support, and to help out when the bride's two hands are not enough. The most successful mother-daughter teams begin the whole process with a sit-down talk, to discuss exactly what's expected in their partnership.

I was a little bit nervous about how my mom would take it when I told her I wanted her role to be limited, but we went out to lunch, just the two of us, and talked it out. She was great.

—Lindsey, bride

ᕙ

Your daughter, too, will be nervous about setting up any parameters, but you can ease her burden by *asking* her exactly what she would like you to do. Have her compose lists in the following categories.

1. Duties that will be solely your responsibility, perhaps booking the limos
2. Tasks she would like your help with, such as choosing her gown, going for fittings, and constructing the guest list
3. Activities that are not your domain, such as planning the honeymoon or choosing the menu

Of course, in the beginning of this process, the bride may not have all of the bases covered. During the wedding's unfolding, issues and tasks will come up that she may not have covered in her original lists, so assure her now that she's free to add, delete, or move things on these lists. This is not a one-time-only contract, and you should not be offended if your daughter chooses to remove one of your responsibilities. Promise her that you'll abide by her wishes, and this is just a step that she can take to assert her own wishes.

Your daughter will appreciate, more than you realize, that you respect her enough to *ask* for this input. With this very preliminary step, you give her the message, loud and clear, that you have no intentions of running her over or overruling her. You are setting a good foundation for your partnership, removing some of her fears, and putting her at ease.

Communication is key, the one thing that will make the planning process go smoothly, that will prevent fights, resentment, and bitterness. It's up to both of you to learn to work together now, even if you never could before. It may not be easy, but for this special time you have to make it work.

To begin with, it's important that you and your daughter establish a time to check in with each other on the issues and tasks that you have to discuss. Avoid becoming a nag, though. Don't call every day with questions, details, and gripes. Respect your daughter's schedule, her down time, and her personal life. Perhaps you can arrange a once-a-week call for updates or questions. (Some moms and daughters communicate via e-mail.) If you agree on the once-a-week schedule, with understood exceptions for emergencies, whether yours or hers, keep a spiral notebook handy in which you can make all your notes. This will be your communications handbook, where you will record everything that needs to be run by your daughter. Having one notebook like this is the best way to be organized and efficient. Date your entries so that all matters can be discussed at the right time. Here, you will also record your daughter's instructions to you.

Communicating With the Bridal Party

Don't be surprised if you land in the position of having to push the bridal party to set deadlines. Those individuals are in the middle of their own lives. They're not in the center of the action, so to speak, so your getting their shoe sizes may not seem urgent to them. All it takes is a quick phone call or a polite note explaining that you're on a deadline and could they please send that information as soon as possible?

≈

Since I didn't want a confrontation, I just called the bridesmaids at home when I knew they'd be at work. I left messages on their machines. It may not be the most efficient way of doing it, but I got my point across, and I didn't have to worry about nagging or coming across like a shrew.
—Nancy, mother of the bride

≈

Issues to Handle With the Bridal Party

Here are some issues about which you may have to communicate with the bridal party, both male and female.

1. The date to select their wardrobes
2. Their sizes and ordering information
3. Payment delivery
4. Their fittings schedules
5. Directions to the tailor
6. Their shoe orders
7. Payment for their shoes
8. Their transportation to the wedding
9. Their lodging plans
10. Their special lodging needs
11. Shower and pre-wedding party plans

Now, there's one thing that all of the women I spoke to agree upon: Don't take anything for granted. Confirm everything. Remind twice. Ask. Tell. Chase. Leave nothing to chance. Don't assume the maids know where to show up for their fittings. Don't assume the men know to get dark socks to wear at the ceremony. It's all these little details that have to get scooped up by somebody, and it may often be you.

It is a good idea to keep detailed notes on who you spoke to and when. If Bridesmaid #3 has not yet paid for her shoes, it may be time for a friendly reminder. Do not complain to the bride that her friends are irresponsible. She probably already knows that, and it will not help her to have you judging her closest, albeit imperfect, friends.

Just do your best to arrange everything and make the phone calls on your own in a tactful, organized way. If the bridal party still does not conform to the schedule, talk to the maid of honor about hurrying things along. In this area, you should respect that there is a maid or matron of honor to assume some responsibility for her peers.

Think of the maid or matron of honor as your underboss. She is there to help out. She has been given this position of honor by your daughter, and as such she has taken on a role of assistant. It is a good idea to establish a friendly, conversational relationship with this member of the bridal party. She can answer many of your questions, and she will be willing to help out with little details you may choose to hand off.

Communicating With the Groom's Family

When dealing with the groom's family, you may have to call on your diplomacy skills. You may have known these people for years. Perhaps they're already family to you. But weddings can do strange things to people. It's important for you to let go of any old traditional thoughts you may have—that the bride's family runs the show, for instance—and try to accommodate the groom's family's wants and needs. Think of it this way: What if it were your son getting married? Wouldn't you feel a little left out of all the planning? Wouldn't you want to add your own personal touches, your own contributions to the whole event? Wouldn't you like to feel that you could put in your say? Just be mindful of their position.

It is a good idea to start the wedding planning process with a friendly conversation with the groom's parents. Perhaps you might take them out to dinner, along with the bride and groom. Choose a nice restaurant with a comfortable, cozy atmosphere, one in which you can talk. Start the evening off with a toast to the bride and groom, and begin discussions about the wedding. This first meeting should have a tone of excitement about the event ahead. It is not the time to whip out a notebook and start assigning tasks. This is just an introduction to your working partnership.

Allow the bride and groom to assume the leadership role in the discussion. Your place may just be to ask questions. Ask them what they envision. Ask them what they want. Offer your assistance and guidance, but leave it up to them to steer the discussion.

In later meetings or talks with the family of the groom, you may choose to bring up details. Of course, you cannot make solid plans until the bride and groom have set the planning wheels in motion. You cannot choose your wardrobe until they decide on a date and degree of formality for the wedding. You cannot plan a guest list until they decide on the size of the wedding.

Bridal guides and bridal magazine articles list the roles and responsibilities of the groom's family as follows.

- Give a congratulations party for the bride and groom, meant as an introduction to their friends. (This is optional.)
- Provide their wedding guest list.
- Check with the bride's family about the wedding wardrobe needs.

- Assume the cost of several wedding expenses, such as marriage license, clergy fees, and so forth.
- Attend all pre-wedding parties and showers.
- Attend the rehearsal and rehearsal dinner.
- Host the rehearsal dinner.
- Sit at the parents' table during the reception.

Of course, as with any of the traditional wedding roles, these duties are optional and subject to shuffling by the bride and groom. It's just best if you know the starting point for the planning. It is a good idea to have the bride and groom let you know what the groom's parents will take on as their responsibility. Be sure to ask in a nonthreatening way, as you do not want the bride to think you are resentful of her giving a particular task to "the other side." Establish now that you are fully willing to work with his parents and that you are making yourself available to them for any assistance they might need.

What if you hate them? Many mothers of brides whom I have spoken to complained about the groom's family's behavior, class level, or general bad behavior. Although it may not be fun to make plans with people who do not adhere to your sense of right versus wrong or class versus trash, remember that these are your daughter's prospective in-laws. She, more than anyone else, must figure out how to deal with them and blend in with them. Be particularly sensitive to your daughter's needs, if this is an issue. She is marrying their son, not them, so keep the focus on how wonderful he is. His family must be involved in the planning of the wedding, and as such you must deal with them on a professional, if not warm, level. It will do the bride no good if you complain to her that the bride's mother is a procrastinator. What can the bride do about that?

In the case of the Runaway Mother of the Groom, when his mother attempts to run the show, it will take some tact on your part to rein her in and keep her from stressing out both you and the bride. You have a partnership with her, and it is your job to establish the boundaries for *both* of your roles. If the mother of the groom takes a hard line with your daughter—as your daughter will most likely be the one whom the mother of the groom contacts with requests and demands—see the power play for what it is. Know that your daughter feels torn between wanting to be assertive and wanting to remain in her future mother-in-law's good graces. Your role as the peacemaker and facilitator of the wedding means that you will have to step into choppy waters to remedy the situation. And how you handle this predicament will color your future relationship with the groom's family.

Take her out to lunch. Discuss with her the pleasure the kids take in planning their wedding. Perhaps you can reach her by using psychology. Tell her that you have your own wishes for certain elements of the wedding, and although it is difficult to let the kids run the show, you know that it is ultimately in their best interest to allow them to agree to or veto any suggestions. Handled carefully, you will not arouse her defensiveness, and the two of you can hold an adult conversation about your roles.

Of course, she may not be as willing as you are to step back and let the bride and groom decide. And if she continues to be difficult, your best bet is to go to your daughter—not to complain, but to allow her to vent her feelings, to make her feel understood and sympathized with.

≷

My mother-in-law doesn't come from a lot of money, and she had a lot of criticism for my parents' ability to spend a lot on the wedding. Every piece of information she got, she called us "hoity-toity" and otherwise made me feel bad. I realized that she was just jealous, and I actually felt sorry for her. We cut her out of the plans and hurt her feelings, but it was her own doing.

—Cindy, bride

≷

Simply deal with the groom's family the best you can, use the Golden Rule, and focus on the larger meaning of the event for all of the wedding planning issues: the celebration of the bride and groom's love. This planning process doesn't last forever, but your continued relationship with his family will go on. You will undoubtedly share grandchildren with these people, so do your best to see the good in them, understand where they're coming from, and help your daughter avoid any power struggles between the two sides.

Communicating With the Groom

The groom is not just an uninvolved bystander. In today's weddings, the groom is extremely involved in most levels of the planning process. Many grooms choose to take on wedding planning responsibilities, such as hiring limousine companies or booking the honeymoon, and in most instances they share equally in the bride's decision-making process on all topics. So you should feel comfortable talking with him as well as with your daughter on the planning front. Remember, his timing and booking styles may be different than your own. It is not your place to instruct him or criticize him.

🐦

My son-in-law decided to design and print the wedding invitations on his home computer. I thought they looked cheap and tacky, but my daughter loved them. Even though I knew the guests would not approve, I just kept my mouth shut. He was, after all, taking a part in his own wedding, and it was not my place to interfere.
—Jeannette, mother of the bride

🐦

What if you hate the groom? More than one set of parents of the bride have had their problems with the man of their daughter's dreams. He may be a slacker, an underachiever, or just someone of a different political or religious persuasion than you. In any case, it's time to give up your judgmental attitude. He is going to be your daughter's husband, and she is making this decision for herself. You will have to trust that she is doing what's right for her. Even if you doubt the long-term prospects of this marriage, it is not your place to attack or criticize him now.

If he is not an abusive alcoholic or in some other way dangerous to your daughter, leave him be. Do not confront your daughter with her fiancé's shortcomings or with any problems you have with his decisions in the wedding. Respect the bride and groom as the adults they are, and let them handle their partnership on their own.

The best thing you can do is consciously try to see the good in him. Look at how happy your daughter is with him. Concentrate on what he does do for her, rather than what you wish he did for her. Keep in mind that your daughter's husband is not all he's going to be yet. He, too, is just starting out on the road of adulthood, and he may have many successes in his future. If he is not perfect now, remember that no one is.

Communicating With the Father of the Bride

Your husband may have some problems with the planning of the wedding. In many cases, they will center around money. If your husband constantly complains about the rising price tag or, worse, blames the bride and groom for not being thrifty in their expenditures, it's time to take him aside and remind him that this wedding is his little girl's big day.

There is a scene in the remake of *Father of the Bride* in which Steve Martin finds himself in jail for having something of a nervous breakdown over the rising costs and roller coaster of details for his daughter Anne's wedding. His understanding wife bails him out, but first makes him apologize for taking away any of his daughter's joy by his ludicrous behavior. While you're unlikely to find your husband thrown in jail over hot dog bun packaging, you are in a position to make your husband see the error of his ways. He might just need a wake-up call to realize that he is indeed ruining the wedding and putting undue pressure on the bride and groom.

The way you handle him will also take diplomacy and your skills at male/female communication. Very often, men take out their frustrations on others while women take out their frustrations on themselves. An entire best-selling *Mars/Venus* book industry revolves around this simple concept. Recognize that your husband is likely to feel fear, loss of control, and undoubtedly panic at losing his little girl. How it manifests is by complaining about money and using that to assert his last bit of control over her.

It would not be a good idea for you to recount his psychological shortcomings, but you could nicely mention that his attitude is bringing everyone down. Assure him that everyone involved in the wedding is trying his or her best to get discounts and spend the money wisely, but this is an investment in one of the biggest moments of your daughter's life. Explain to him that your daughter has dreamed of her wedding day since she was old enough to play make-believe, and now the two of you have the ability to make her lifetime of dreams come true.

That ought to take care of him.

Or the other end of the spectrum is the macho dad who can't bring himself to participate in the wedding. He may want to, but he's not going to ask. You can draw him in and get him to give his input. Make him a part of the process. He'll appreciate it later.

Communicating With Troublemakers

Of course, there will always be that one person who drives you up a wall. It could be your own sister, your cousin, or the groom's brother. So many people will have opinions and comments to share. They'll criticize you, your daughter, your daughter's in-laws, and your plans for the wedding. Etiquette-bound mavens may descend upon your decisions and your daughter's. Ego-deflated relatives may attack in an effort to make themselves feel superior.

A wedding brings out the best and worst in all people. People respond to a major life change event in another person's life as if it is a statement about their own lives. Divorced friends may question the validity of marriage, even going so far as to say, "I give this marriage six months." In many ways, the people around you may vent their frustrations at life in the general direction of your daughter's happiness.

Brides and other mothers of brides advise you now: *Just take a deep breath. Walk away if you have to, but just let it go. The important thing, the only important thing right then, is that your daughter is getting married. Don't let the presence of a complete jerk take any part of that joy away from you.* Feel sorry for a person who cannot simply appreciate life. Some people do not have a capacity for happiness, and they don't want others to be happy either. Recognize that message for what it is, and deflect any attacks from people with less than generous motives.

Communicating With Professionals

When dealing with any professional—say your daughter asks you to book a photographer or just needs some guidance while doing it herself—you have a great responsibility. In many ways, the correct choice of wedding professionals makes the wedding. Your guests will remember the quality of the food and the entertainment, and the wedding photos and video are your timeless reminders of the celebration. Choose wisely now. Do your homework and make the best choice of professionals with solid credentials and glowing reviews to prove their worthiness to participate in your daughter's wedding.

Which professionals are we talking about? The list goes beyond caterers and DJs. You will be dealing with a great number of professionals who are part of a $3.2 billion wedding industry in the United States. The professionals you will consider fall under the categories below.

- ◆ Wedding coordinators
- ◆ Clergy, if not affiliated with your church or synagogue
- ◆ Ring sales managers

- Bridal salon clerks
- Tailors and seamstresses
- Tuxedo rental clerks
- Caterers
- Banquet hall managers
- Bakers
- Ice sculpture artists
- Limousine company managers and drivers
- DJs or bands
- Photographers
- Videographers
- Ethnic specialty performers
- Travel agents
- Hotel managers

As in any profession, there are good eggs and bad eggs, and your legwork now will weed out the bad choices and unearth the gems. Here are a few tips for making the right choices.

1. Do your research. Look through the Yellow Pages, analyze ads, call for brochures. Gather as much hard information as you can on the business or service, and use that to eliminate bad choices and elevate good choices.
2. Ask your friends. Whom did they hire to do their daughter's wedding? Did that person do a good job? Can you see their wedding pictures, for instance? Your best bet is to go with a pro who's already proven himself to people you trust.
3. Make charts. Compare and contrast your final choices, making notes like "said he would throw in all the proofs for free." These tidbits will aid your final decision.
4. Get samples. Taste the baker's wedding cake. Look at the florist's roses and stephanotises. Watch a sample videotape done by the videographer. See what the

final result will be. Don't just take the professional's word for it. He's not going to say, "I do a mediocre job, but what do you want for the money I'm charging you?"

5. Get it in writing. All aspects of your agreement should be in writing. If it's the photographer you're dealing with, get exact measurements of the prints you will order, exact numbers of albums, payment plan options, and so forth. Get it all in writing, date it, and make sure you get the name of the person who made the contract with you. Keep a copy of your contract.

6. Check with the Better Business Bureau to see if this company has had any complaints charged against it. Go with companies that have clear track records.

7. Go for the discount. Perhaps you can talk your way into getting something for free, or obtaining a discount on your large order. It can't hurt to ask.

8. Confirm, confirm, confirm. Call a month ahead of time to be sure they've ordered the gowns. Call a week ahead of time to confirm, say, the limos. Call the reception hall manager the night before. Write down the dates and times you called, as well as with whom you spoke. There's no such thing as being too sure when it comes to successfully coordinating all of the many little details of a wedding. You'd rather be safe than left out on the curb waiting for limos.

9. Keep documentation. Be organized. Most mothers of brides have a shoebox or a folder for their contracts and brochures, in order to keep everything in one place. You'll be amazed at the pile of papers that will accumulate, so it's in your best interest to be able to find what you need. Sample worksheets are provided in chapters 5 and 6.

10. Follow up afterward. Send a note if you liked the service. Send a note if you didn't. If the service was a complete failure and you want your money back, don't hesitate to ask. You have your documentation and contracts, saved and organized; you know whom you talked to and when; you know when you confirmed. You're in good shape for a refund.

11. Remember to check back with the bride. Make sure you have her directions clear, and that she's okay with the actions you're taking.

If you haven't caught on to the theme by now, it's that you are the communications center of the wedding. In many ways, it is you who will keep the wheels turning, keep everyone on track, and smooth over the rough spots of your daughter's wedding planning process. You have tremendous power to prevent many of the problems that stress out brides, alienate family members, and create headaches that take away from the joy of the event.

Remember that half of communication is listening. In listening, you can uncover the hidden meanings behind people's words, know where their gripes are coming from, and give the bride what she needs most: understanding and support.

∂⊘

When dealing with others, all I ask is that the mother of the bride just LISTEN to everybody.

—Karen, bride

∂⊘

On pages 24–25, you will find an invaluable tool to help organize the wedding. It is a master list of contact information for everyone with whom you will communicate during the wedding planning process. Fill in the addresses and phone numbers for all players in the wedding plans—don't forget work numbers, too!

Contact List

Bride _____

Groom _____

Maid/matron of honor _____

Best man _____

Bridesmaids _____

_____

_____

_____

_____

Ushers _____

_____

_____

_____

_____

Flower girl's parents _____

Ring bearer's parents _____

Groom's parents _____

Dress shop _____

Seamstress _____

Shoe store _____

Tuxedo rentals _____

Wedding officiant _____

Musical performers _____

Florist _____

Caterer _____

DJ/band _____

Photographer _____

Videographer _____

Limos _____

Others _____

_____

_____

_____

3

The Budget

LET'S GET RIGHT TO IT: the cold, hard cash. Face it, money is a deciding factor in every wedding. The budget dictates the size of the wedding, the formality, the menu, and every other possible element of the celebration. And when money is involved, many other issues can arise as well.

As mentioned earlier, brides of previous eras found their weddings controlled by those who held the purse strings, usually their parents. Less enlightened parents exerted control over decisions by saying (or implying), "I'm paying for it, so I make the call." Today, brides and grooms have their own incomes, so the issue of who pays for what is not so clear-cut.

The etiquette books outline the traditional "Who Pays" charts according to the following accepted model, but again, it's up to the individual couples and their families to assign financial responsibilities all around.

❧

Who Pays for What—The Traditional Model

The Bride's Family

- Invitations and announcements
- Wedding programs
- Wedding gown and accessories
- Reception site
- Reception menu
- Flowers
- Photographer
- Videographer
- Entertainment
- Transportation
- Lodging for guests

The Groom's Family

- Marriage license
- Wedding officiant
- The bride's bouquet
- The groom's and usher's boutonnieres
- The rehearsal dinner
- The honeymoon

Of course, this is just the traditional model, and very few people follow it precisely anymore. Today's loosened wedding standards mean that there is always room for discussion about who will assume which expenditures.

The best course of action is to sit down with the bride and groom to discuss what they would like to pay for. The best handling of this conversation is the starter, "We'd like to help out wherever you'd like, so just let us know what you want." The average bride and groom will appreciate your flexibility, and you will undoubtedly receive a good response. They will at this time say whether or not they've decided to foot the whole bill, and you might hear about the groom's family's similar offer.

Here's where you must remove your ego from the situation. If the groom's family would like to pay for the videographer, for example, you must not see that offer as an encroachment on your rights as the bride's parents. Understand their intentions as just wanting to help out.

Too many families of brides and grooms fight over money issues, creating undue stress and placing the bride and groom in the middle of what eventually becomes an all-out war. It may be that the groom's family has more money than yours, but their offer shouldn't be interpreted as some sort of insult to you. His family just wants to help create a beautiful day for the couple.

Handling this issue well at the outset will prevent hard feelings that will mar the wedding and create a lasting schism between your family and his. Explain to your daughter, perhaps when she is away from her fiancé, that you would love to handle whatever finances possible. She should just state her wishes.

If the bride and groom decide to pay for the wedding themselves, this is not the time to flex your muscles. You may mean well when you say, "But you could have a much better wedding if we paid for everything"; however, the bride and groom will only be offended. It is their decision, and they know what they're doing. It may very well be that they run out of money halfway through the planning—wedding budgets nearly always surpass planned boundaries—and in that instance, they may choose to come to you. Giving them an "I told you so" will only diminish them, so hold back your commentary—and open your checkbook.

After a good discussion with the bride and groom, you will understand your budget responsibilities. You will know who is taking care of what. The most important thing now is to remove the control from the money. You may be footing the bill for the flowers, but that does not mean that you get to overrule your daughter's decision on which blooms to buy. This is often very difficult for most parents. For most of your life, money has meant power. And although you may not like to admit it, it has meant power over your children. You handed out an allowance, you taught your children to save their money, you may have commented when they frittered away their savings on clothes and CDs. Now, your judgments must stop. You have graciously offered to foot the bill for whatever the bride and groom choose.

Money scares people. Your daughter and her fiancé may be frightened at the size of the bill for the wedding they envision. They may feel bad about burdening you, his parents, or even themselves with the great expense, especially if they know that there is a money crunch in the family. Here again, you'll have to assuage your daughter's fears about money. Let her know that although there are limits to what can be spent, she shouldn't reduce herself to a quivering wreck over it.

It broke my heart to hear my daughter say, after her wedding, that she felt she really ripped herself off in an effort to save us money. We thought she was just being frugal—it turned out she was undercutting her dreams to save us money.

—Leigh, mother of the bride

You may have heard frightening statistics about wedding budgets. The average wedding today costs more than $20,000. Joan Rivers just spent $1,000,000 on the wedding she gave for her daughter, Melissa. Don't scare yourself with big money stories. Look at the elements of the budget in individual terms and set a workable dollar amount for each expenditure.

The bride's priorities will establish how much is to be spent on each thing. She may want a glamorous Vera Wang wedding gown, so you will shift a larger percentage of the wedding budget to that element. She may not care to hire limousines, so money for that expense can be shifted to the caterer's bill. Each wedding is unique, and its components are entirely up to the bride and groom. Ask the bride to establish her priorities. She should list the biggest budget categories so that you know where to devote the financial weight.

Use the chart on pages 30–31 to establish a beginner budget—that is, your beginning estimate of what will be spent where. Cross off the items that will be handled by the groom's family, as their budget is their responsibility. In the far-right column, you can record actual prices, once you've done some homework.

Beginning Budget

Item	Amount Budgeted	Actual Amount
Engagement party		
Engagement gift		
Wedding gown		
Wedding gown accessories		
Tuxedos		
Ceremony site fee		
Officiant fee		
Musicians for the ceremony		
Throwaways for the ceremony		
Candles		
Invitations		
Announcements		
Newspaper announcement fee		
Reception site		
Reception menu		
Beverages		
Cake		

Item	Amount Budgeted	Actual Amount
Entertainment		
Photographer		
Videographer		
Limousines		
Transportation		
Lodging		
Your wedding wardrobe		
Your wedding accessories		
Other children's wedding wardrobe		
Toasting flutes		
Cake knife		
Favors		
Wedding license		
Honeymoon		
Other expenses		

Total up the amounts, and see where your money stands.

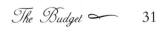

Stretching the Budget by Finding Savings

Perhaps the best way to handle a wedding budget is to stretch it. In my book *1001 Ways to Save Money and Still Have a Dazzling Wedding,* I explain how to have a beautiful wedding on a bargain-basement budget. I've interviewed hundreds of brides and their families and found that the most beautiful of weddings have been celebrated for just a fraction of what the average wedding costs. With a little bit of effort, big savings can be found for every wedding expense.

As with all things, moderation is key. It is possible to get many wedding services and items for free—through bartering your own professional expertise in exchange for a wedding professional's services or accepting free services as a wedding gift from one of your guests—but you should not go overboard. Sometimes if a price is too good to be true, it is the porthole to a world of headaches. The key is finding smart savings, being a good consumer, and asking for discounts wherever possible.

The following are some of the main money-saving ideas that have expanded wedding budgets all over the country.

The Basics

- Smaller is cheaper. The fewer people you invite, the less you will spend.
- Less formal is cheaper. An ultraformal affair will run you anywhere from $100 to $500 per person. Included in that cost are menu fees for lobster tails and filet mignon, extensive liquors and after-dinner drinks, desserts, and so forth. A garden tea party, in contrast, means appetizers and other less-expensive entrees. The average tea party runs $25 to $50 per person, depending upon the menu choices made.
- Choose your location with price in mind. The most expensive, most formal location in your town will run you more money than a beautiful site of lesser star-value.
- Keep the season in mind. A Valentine's Day wedding is romantic, but the elevated cost of flowers at that time will affect your budget.

Engagement Party

- Research your options. It may be cheaper, and more cozy, to have the engagement party in your home with a catered menu than to have a smaller version of a wedding at a banquet hall.
- Get the liquor at a discount wholesaler. You can find these listed in the Yellow Pages.
- Choose your own china and flatware over a stock of rented finery.
- Make it a coffee and dessert party, with a wide selection of luscious cakes and petit fours, rather than a full buffet dinner.
- Skip the hired musicians. Just leave music on the CD player, and ask a relative or friend to play DJ for the night.

Reception Locations

- Choose a reception location that already has chairs and tables. Renting these necessary objects will cost big.
- An outdoor setting means a big price tag for rentals, power generators, tents, and so on. It may seem like a cheaper idea, but the expenses add up.
- Consider a winery, an arboretum, or another unique location. In many cases, rental fees will be lower.
- Keep location fees and permits in mind. These are often hidden expenses, so you need to know what you're dealing with.

Religious Elements

- Find out ahead of time what is allowed and what is not. You will lose your deposit for the string quartet if you find out later they are not permitted to perform in the church.
- Save money on an aisle runner, a chuppah, or a unity candle by making them yourself or accepting them as gifts from special relatives.
- Clear your idea for post-wedding toss-its, such as birdseed or the release of butterflies. The church or synagogue probably has rules about that, and not

clearing the idea first could mean a waste of money . . . and butterflies that don't get to fly away.

The Gown

- Allow plenty of time to look around. Most wedding experts advise a year for the appropriate comparison-shopping time. A rush order may mean getting an expensive gown and having to pay extra for hurried delivery and alterations.
- Do not allow the bride to order a dress she hasn't tried on. Every gown has its own fit, and ordering out of a catalog is a big mistake—especially if you have to buy a second gown.
- Get bridal magazines from the library, and use the designers' toll-free numbers to request catalogs or ordering information for the most-loved designs.
- Check out smaller bridal salons. These businesses have less overhead, so their prices may be cheaper.
- Check out the dresses in the bridal sections of major department stores.
- Buy a simpler, more classic gown. All of the ornate beading is expensive—as you're paying for hand-sewn extras.
- Buy a gown in a less expensive material. Comparison shop among pressed cotton, satin, taffeta, and so forth.
- If the gown on a rack at the salon has a fixable flaw, ask for a discount.
- Ask the salon manager when the next shipment of gowns will arrive. With advance notice, you may be able to beat the crowd to find the most affordable one.
- Use a credit card when paying for the gown. This is proof of purchase and will protect you in case there is a problem.
- Comparison shop for alteration fees.
- Check out bridal shows for discounts, designers, and even the possibility of winning a free gown as a door prize.

Shoes and Accessories

- Don't pay extra for new shoes. Both you and the bride can use shoes you already have—if the style and color are appropriate—and you won't have to worry about breaking in new shoes or getting blisters.
- Don't order shoes at a bridal salon. Try a discount shoe store instead.
- The bride may be able to get her shoes for free if you place the order within the bulk order of the bridesmaids shoes. Hers just don't get dyed.
- Look for seasonal shoe sales.
- See if the bride is interested in wearing your veil. That can be a $300 savings. It can be cleaned and altered for her style.
- Have a talented friend or relative make the veil.
- Don't allow the bride to buy new jewelry to wear with her gown. Most likely, you or the groom will gift her with jewels for the wedding day.
- For your own jewelry, wear the best, most appropriate pieces you already own.

Bridal Party Wardrobe

- Encourage the bridesmaids to choose a gown according to their budget, not yours.
- Encourage them to choose a simpler, more elegant style.
- Encourage them to choose a style that they can wear again. Long skirts can be cut short.
- When renting tuxedos, ask for the groom's or the father of the bride's tux for free.

Your Wardrobe

- Choose a simple, elegant style that does not compete with your daughter's gown.
- Visit outlets and department store sales.
- Shop after major holidays.

Invitations

- Know exactly how many invitations you'll need so that you don't order too many.
- Order small invitations, as opposed to oversize ones, to save on postage.
- Order lighter (thinner) paper types to save on postage.
- Choose simpler styles in black on beige, rather than colored or textured ones.
- Choose the less-expensive thermographed styles over the engraved.
- Be careful with the wording and spelling of your invitations. Any mistakes will call for a reprinting at extra expense. (Any mistakes made by the printer will be corrected free of charge—do not let them bully you into paying for it. Check for errors when you pick up the invitations.)
- Experienced graphic artists can design the invitations for you. Let it be their wedding gift. Then take them to a quality copy shop for duplications.
- Make sure all invitations are addressed correctly and that your addresses are up to date, so that none are returned to you for a second sending.
- If a map is needed, design it on a home computer for inclusion in the invitation package.

Rings

- Use your family's regular jeweler for proven reliability.
- Check discount jewelry stores.
- If you have a friend in the business, try to use his employee discount.
- Choose a jeweler who offers free engraving and sizing.
- Choose plain bands over detailed bands.
- Choose wedding band sets over individual styles.
- Always buy a ring with a good warranty.
- Get the rings appraised immediately.

Flowers and Decor

- Ask the officiant if the site will be decorated already. For instance, holiday weddings can make use of the poinsettias already in place at the church.
- Ask the officiant about rules regarding floral decor. If you find out on the wedding day that no flowers can be set up, your $2,000-worth of flowers will be sitting in the back of a van.
- Use your family's regular florist for proven reliability.
- Order flowers that are in season. Out-of-season blooms are expensive to ship in from overseas.
- Order more common flowers, not the exotic ones that cost $5 per stem.
- Use more greenery in bouquets and centerpieces.
- Consider one long-stemmed rose per bridesmaid.
- Learn to make bouquets, corsages, and boutonnieres yourself with flowers you buy loose at a discount florist.
- Bypass the delivery fee and pick up the flowers yourself on the wedding day.
- Don't order rose petals for the flower girl to drop on her way down the aisle. If you want this effect, have a relative give you flowers from her own garden, and pull the petals from those.
- Skip the pricy centerpieces on pedestals. Smaller flower arrangements or bowls of floating candles are elegant, and the guests can see each other across the table.

Transportation

- Comparison shop like crazy.
- Call the National Limousine Association at 800-NLA-7007 for referrals and ratings of limo companies.
- Get just one limo, for the bride and groom. Ship the bridal party in a decorated minivan, or ask the hotel if you can use their free shuttle.
- Don't bother ordering champagne to be stocked in the limo. You can find a less-expensive bottle yourself, or the bride and groom can wait until the reception before the toasting begins.

Photographer and Videographer

- Get referrals from friends who were happy with their photographers and videographers.
- Always look at samples of their work.
- Again, comparison shop like crazy.
- Consider the packages. Many packages offer discounts for copies. Think ahead as to how many albums, enlargements, and copies you will really need, but do not purchase a package that is too expensive. Remember, your guests will probably give you copies of their photos, too.
- Ask the photographer if you get the proofs for free.
- Get a percentage of the photos in black and white. It's a classic look, and it's cheaper.
- Have experienced friends take pictures and videos at the wedding.
- Just have the photographer shoot the ceremony and the beginning of the reception—the first dance, the toast, and so forth. Candid shots can take care of the rest of the night.

The Menu

- Get samples. Always taste the food you'll serve to your guests. The menu is the biggest reception expense, so you want to be sure you get your money's worth.
- Choose a menu that is appropriate for the season.
- Don't go into overkill with the appetizers. At most ornate weddings, guests commented that there was just too much, and many were too full after the cocktail hour to eat their meals.
- Avoid expensive foods like lobster and caviar. Gourmet dishes of lesser expense will be appreciated just the same.
- Limit the extra desserts. By the end of the evening, people are so full they hardly even touch their wedding cake.
- Skip the international coffee bar. It's not a necessity, and plain coffee will work fine for most people.

- If you'll be preparing the food, shop in bulk.
- Offer a narrow selection of liquors—perhaps just beer, wine, champagne, and soft drinks. Providing a fully stocked bar means a higher price per person.
- Close the bar early. It's better for the expense and for the safety of your guests.

Entertainment

- Check out price per hour versus flat fee.
- Hiring a DJ may not mean live versions of the music you like, but it also means feeding one person, rather than the twelve members of a band.
- Ask if the reception hall can pipe classical or easy-listening music into the room.
- Consider renting a jukebox for an informal wedding.
- For late-night fun, hook up your own karaoke machine or borrow a friend's.

The Cake

- Don't order through the bridal salon's or caterer's referral.
- Use your own tried-and-true bakery for proven reliability.
- Ask for free delivery.
- Take 10 percent off your total head count when ordering the cake. Not everyone eats cake at the reception.
- Order a simple cake that you can decorate yourself with (safe) flowers and blooms.
- Allow a talented relative to make the cake for you, especially for an informal wedding.
- Make the groom's cake yourself.
- Skip the groom's cake.

Favors

- Shop at discount craft stores for simple favor ideas.
- Have a friend make the favors as her gift to the bride and groom.

- Make a donation to a favorite charity in lieu of favors. Provide a printed announcement for placement at the guests' seats.

Lodging

- Ask for group rates.
- With a big order, the honeymoon suite may be negotiated for free.
- Skip the honeymoon suite for the first night. A regular room, decorated for the bride and groom, is just as wonderful.
- Allow out-of-town guests to stay at nearby relatives' homes.

The Honeymoon

- Suggest a non-honeymoon destination for cheaper rates.
- Book flights for off-peak hours.
- Find out if relatives in the business can swing a discount.
- Cash in frequent flyer miles.
- Check your auto club's discounts and special trips.

Personal Beauty Care

- Book a discount bridal party package at the salon for the morning of the wedding. Hair and nails can be done at a discount, and the bride may get her treatments for free.

Of course, there are countless ways to save money while booking the wedding. The most important universal concepts are:

1. Asking for discounts
2. Asking for group rates
3. Keeping good records and keeping track of deposits
4. Paying with credit cards for proof of purchase
5. Allowing talented relatives and friends to offer their services as their gift to the couple

6. Comparison shopping
7. Avoiding too-good-to-be-true services and sales
8. Getting referrals
9. Checking Web sites and resources for free items and discounts (see Resource sections at the back of this book)

Do-It-Yourself Hints

You can save a lot of money by using your crafting skills and talents. If you intend to make favors, pew bows, or even the bride's veil, check with the bride and groom as you make your plans and buy your materials, and throughout the craft process. It's wonderful that you're contributing in this way. It lends a personalized touch to the wedding.

Here are some ideas for do-it-yourself options.

- Design the wedding invitations, the wedding program, or the map on your home computer.
- Sew the bride's veil.
- Make the bride's cash/gift bag.
- Sew the pillow for the ring bearer's use.
- Make the unity candle.
- Make the aisle runner and the pew bows.
- Make the bouquets, corsages, boutonnieres, and centerpieces.
- Bake the wedding cake.
- Prepare some, if not all, of the wedding food.
- Design the place cards or handwrite them.
- Assemble the post-ceremony toss-its: pretty baskets of flower petals, birdseed, and so forth.
- Put together the favors.

Homemade Favor Ideas

Scented candles
Chocolates
Scented soaps
Books of poetry
Party bags
Baked goods
Music mixes
Beauty products
Gift certificates to eateries
Silver frames containing poetry or a
  picture of the couple

Seedlings or bulbs
Potpourri in glass bowls
Mini photo albums
Breakfast in a bag (for the next
  morning): bagels, jellies, juices
Homemade wine from your own
  "winery"
Edited videotapes of the couple's
  love story
Bubble baths
Gift certificates to salons

Tipping Guidelines

Tips can add up. Don't forget to factor in the tips when figuring out the wedding budget. Here is a list of the most common tipping rules.

- Banquet hall manager: 10–20 percent of the total reception bill
- Bartenders: 10 percent of the liquor bill
- Beauty consultants: 15–20 percent of beauty salon bill
- Coat check: $1 per guest
- DJ or band: $20–$30 each, depending on quality of performance
- Delivery people: $10–20 each
- Limousine driver: 15–20 percent of total transportation bill
- Party bus or van driver: $20–$40, depending on number of trips
- Wedding consultant: 10–15 percent of wedding expense (if all goes well)

4

The Guest List

ONE OF THE MOST IMPORTANT DECISIONS to make in planning a wedding is the size of the guest list. This is a key factor in future decisions, as it plays a part in determining the reception location, the menu choices, the number of favors, and just about every other aspect of the plans. Planning a guest list is nothing new to you—you did this for your own wedding. What is different now is that, as the mother of the bride, your role is quite different than that of the bride.

Your main role here is to help the bride plan the guest list for her wedding. While you are bound by the constraints of budget and head count, constructing a guest list means walking a fine line between Have Tos and Shoulds. What this means is that you are dealing with family relations. You have many relatives whom you may want to attend the wedding, and if there is no room on the list for 200 people from your side alone, some cuts will have to be made. That means possibly offending people. But you know, probably much better than your daughter does, who in the family _must_ be invited.

The bride is well aware of the restraints on the guest list, and she has a wish list of her own. She, of course, would rather have her college roommates at the wedding than great-aunts who are close to you but not close to her. Together, you and the bride will have to sit down and find a way to make the guest list work.

Here is a good way to start. Make a date with the bride and groom for the compilation of your half of the guest list. By now, the bride and groom have decided that they want either a small or a large wedding, so you know where to begin.

The best way to create your list is to break down your guests into Have Tos and Maybes. Create two different lists, using the appropriate pages at the end of this chapter. Have Tos are grandparents, aunts, uncles, cousins, friends, and other important people whom neither of you would dream of cutting from the list. They are your closest relatives, friends, and colleagues. On the Maybe list, write people whom you would love to invite if you could.

Where do you make cuts if the guest list gets out of control? Many brides report that they draw a line after first cousins. All extended family members simply cannot be added. Protecting fragile egos is an important part of your role. You will have to explain to people that you simply cannot invite everyone you'd love to have at the wedding. What you might find, in the case of distant family members and other only-so-close people whom you know, is that they understand. They may even have several other weddings to attend that season and feel relieved not to have to travel.

Understand at this time that it is the bride and groom's wedding. They want to share the day with their friends and coworkers. Too many brides have complained after the wedding that they wished they had stood firmer about inviting more of their friends.

ðŸ‚Š

I had to leave off some of my college friends, and now they're not talking to me. I wasn't invited to their weddings. All because my parents had to invite THEIR friends and clients.

—Dara, bride

ðŸ‚Š

The rationale provided by parents of brides whose guest lists were commandeered is that their clients and friends are older, more established, and would give the couple better gifts. Think about that. Does the bride want her friends at the wedding, in the conga line, and in great candid photos that she will display in her home forever, or does she want a Lalique candy dish? Don't worry about the quality of the wedding gifts. Make room on the guest list for the bride's and groom's favorite people.

If the bride and groom know and are close to your clients and coworkers, then ask them if these people might be added to the list. Without using a guilt trip, add them to the Maybe list for inclusion if Have Tos cannot attend. That is the essence of compromise.

Another factor in determining the head count is allowing for single wedding guests to bring their significant others. Etiquette books say that only engaged and married couples should be allowed to bring their partners, but in real life the etiquette books can cause more headaches than anything else. The best approach is to write "And Guest" only on the invitations of single guests who are involved in serious relationships. You don't want to pay $200 for a sixteen-year-old niece to bring her boyfriend of one week. Allow guests only for those who are known to be solidly involved.

The bride's input on the list should be paramount. You may feel strongly about wanting your best friend to be present at the wedding, but when every person counts, the bride will want to choose her best friends over yours. Allow her the final decisions, and be understanding when she nixes your coworkers. The greatest mistake you could make at this early stage in the planning process is to dominate the guest list. This means, hold back on imposing your wishes and understand that the bride and groom want to be surrounded by their loved ones.

Remember, this is not your wedding.

With that understood, you are in a good position to support the bride and groom as they create their guest list. You are an invaluable tool, as you will likely supply them with the names, addresses, and phone numbers of the relatives. Be prepared for tension to arise in the bride. Since this is one of the first big jobs, and a difficult one at that, she may be overwhelmed by the issues that come up.

You can help the most by staying away from these common Mom-isms:

1. "But we have to invite them. They came to my wedding."
2. "You were in their bridal party."
3. "She was like an aunt to you as you were growing up."
4. "If we invite them, then we have to invite these other people."
5. "They are going to be so offended if we don't invite them."

Your daughter is an adult. She knows who needs to be there and who doesn't. Pressuring for the people you want at the wedding will only make this job more difficult for her, and if history is any model you will be cut out of the process altogether. Your job, remember, is to make things easier.

Assure the bride that this is just a preliminary list. Don't count as you're writing names down. Allow her to write down as many as possible, and allow her to make her own decisions without any commentary from you. Think of it as your job to make sure that any important people are not left off the list.

In most planning sessions, the parents of the bride and the parents of the groom are asked for their proposed guest list. Usually, a limit is established, say twenty-five or fifty people. The best approach for you is to make your list ahead of time and give it to the bride. Undoubtedly, you will have some duplicate names on your list and hers. As you cross the names off your list, here is where you can earn big points with the bride.

Once you are satisfied with your list, that's it. If new slots open up, do not attempt to fill them with other people you'd like to come. Give those slots to the bride for her to invite her own friends. Make it a priority that the bride can invite her selections, and she will be grateful to you.

What if the budget simply does not allow for a large list? Establish a head count and work with the bride to make all Have Tos fit. Some financially challenged families change the formality of the wedding—switching it to the less-expensive garden tea party—so that a larger number of guests can attend. Discuss that option with the bride. Explain to her that it is a viable solution to the problem. If she is unwilling to change her plans for a formal affair, then the limited guest list sticks.

The groom's family's list should be discussed ahead of time, preferably with the groom. Since he is involved in the planning process, he will understand the trouble you're having fitting your Have Tos into the allowed slots. This is not the time to pressure the groom into getting his parents to give up their slots or to question whether or not his parents' choices are appropriate. You agreed that they should have a certain number of slots, and they are free to fill them up with as many guests as fit comfortably.

In some cases, the groom's family is from another state or even another country. If their guests are unable to travel, they might voluntarily limit their guest list appropriately. But do not count on this. Go through the motions, with an understanding that all of the groom's guest list slots will be used.

Do not invite people just because you believe that they will not be able to come. Too many people do this, expecting to receive a rejection in the mail, and then all of those expected Nos turn into Yesses. The result is an overbooked wedding and a truly gigantic problem. Be realistic at the outset.

After much thinking, shuffling, and compromising, you will eventually create the perfect Have To guest list. Your Maybe guest list should be prioritized so that fill-ins can easily be added without the need for another powwow and further discussion and argument. Rank your Maybes now, for easier inclusion in the Have To list.

Believe me, the bride does not want this job to be stressful. She does not want to worry about anyone's hurt feelings, and she doesn't want to be steamrolled into inviting guests who are not close to her. She should not feel that the wedding is your party and her guests are just add-ons.

Here are some ideas for limiting your guest list.

1. You don't HAVE to invite anyone you don't want there. So leave off unfriendly neighbors, even though you know they'll see the wedding party on the morn-

ing of the wedding. This is the bride's and groom's day, and not everyone can attend.

2. Think twice about allowing couples to bring their kids to the reception. While it is charming to have the kids dancing with the bride and groom, they will certainly get bored during the five hours of the reception, and bored children cause a commotion.

3. Do NOT allow people to bring uninvited guests, even if they write it in on the response card. Their rudeness shouldn't preclude you from being able to invite the guests the couple wants at the wedding.

4. Don't feel pressured to allow teens and unmarried people to bring dates, unless they are engaged or close to the family. While teens are pack animals at heart, they will survive the night without their two-week steadies.

5. The correct wording on your invitation will let people know they cannot bring dates.

6. If anything unexpected shows up on a response card, such as an added escort, call the offender and explain, "We simply do not have room for any extra people."

Use the lists provided on the following pages as templates for assembling your guest list.

The Parents' of the Bride's Personal Guest List

Your guest wish-list, to be handed in for the bride and groom's consideration

1. _____
2. _____
3. _____
4. _____
5. _____
6. _____
7. _____
8. _____
9. _____
10. _____
11. _____
12. _____
13. _____
14. _____
15. _____
16. _____
17. _____
18. _____
19. _____
20. _____

The Groom's Family's Guest List

To be handed in for the bride and groom's consideration

1. _____
2. _____
3. _____
4. _____
5. _____
6. _____
7. _____
8. _____
9. _____
10. _____
11. _____
12. _____
13. _____
14. _____
15. _____
16. _____
17. _____
18. _____
19. _____
20. _____

The Bride's and Groom's Guest List

1. _____
2. _____
3. _____
4. _____
5. _____
6. _____
7. _____
8. _____
9. _____
10. _____
11. _____
12. _____
13. _____
14. _____
15. _____
16. _____
17. _____
18. _____
19. _____
20. _____

Master List with Responses

	Name and Address	Number of People	Attending?
1.			
2.			
3.			
4.			
5.			
6.			
7.			
8.			
9.			
10.			
11.			
12.			
13.			
14.			
15.			
16.			
17.			
18.			
19.			
20.			

Additional Entries

Officiant _____

Ceremony Musician _____

Photogapher _____

Videographer _____

DJ or Band (Include number in band/assistant) _____

Guest Seating Chart

Your caterer and baker will need to know the number of guests who will attend. Your florist or the person making the centerpieces has to know how many tables you need, how you will seat your guests, and what arrangements need to be made. The caterer herself needs to know how the room must be set up, so you should think about the best table placement for the room and how you will arrange your guests.

The table placement issue can easily be taken up with the banquet hall manager. With a solid head count, he or she can tell you which kinds of tables will work best. The head table will most likely be the standard long rectangle, but you may have your choice whether to use round, oval, or rectangular tables for seating your guests, depending on what options are offered to you.

The best bet is to see the room as it is laid out in its standard configuration. Ask the banquet hall manager to allow you to view the setup when it is arranged to nearly your number of guests. Take a walk through and make sure the tables can be set to your liking.

Then it's time to put the guests at the tables.

A piece of advice from all brides and grooms and parents of brides and grooms: Take your time on this one. Think it through. Seating is another one of those prime fight issues, and many a bride and mother have gone for days not talking because of a seating chart situation.

So make many photocopies of this chart, play around, and *do it in pencil*. Or, use a cork bulletin board, write your guests' names on strips of paper (or photocopy your master guest list and cut it into strips), and pin them up against the chart for easier moving and rearranging.

Some issues to keep in mind:

1. Don't seat divorced or divorcing couples together.
2. Don't seat a divorced person with all happy couples.
3. Don't seat sworn enemies together.
4. Don't seat people who owe money together with those to whom they owe.
5. Don't seat the alcoholics right next to the bar.
6. Don't corner your elderly guests in hard-to-reach seats.
7. Put your livelier, dancing guests right next to the dance floor.
8. Seat children with their parents, not at a kiddies' table.
9. Seat similar people together, such as clients, neighbors, second-cousins, and so forth.
10. Have two head tables: one for the parents and grandparents, and one for honored guests.

People are strange. They get very offended if someone is seemingly "ranked higher" than they are at a wedding, so many brides now choose to do away with numbered tables. Too many guests have complained that they were not respected enough to sit in the top three tables, and they mope through the wedding because someone else was ranked higher. You can assuage these delicate egos by giving your tables names instead. Many brides have christened the tables with such nice thoughts as Love, Peace, Joy, Cupid, Eternity, and so on. This simple move saves a mountain of headaches.

One thing to keep in mind when arranging table seating charts is that people will seat themselves at the table on their own, unless you take it upon yourself to give them exact seating. For the most part, it is a wise idea just to specify who goes at which table. Leave the nit-picking to the guests.

Some headaches to expect:

- The girlfriend of an usher wants to sit at the head table, even though she's not a member of the bridal party. Your answer: Tough.
- A difficult old great-aunt is not happy with her seat in the back of the room. Ask if some kind soul will switch with her.
- Some people will want to switch tables on their own. If you see a scuffle breaking out, send the banquet hall manager over to take care of it.

As far as making an individual seating chart, the bride and groom may simply not be aware of many of the family dynamics that exist. In their efforts to make a seating chart on their own, they may inadvertently seat two people together who shouldn't be in the same state, let alone at the same table. Here is where you come in to save the day. Hand the bride and groom the chart on page 56 so that they are made aware of the kinds of situations to avoid. Just make sure your reasons are legitimate and not so picayune that the issue isn't really that important. You may choose to make a copy of this chart for the groom's parents to use, so that their unspoken family dynamics are not made into a big deal. It is simply to be used to assist the bride and groom with the task.

If the bride and groom ask for your advice on the seating chart, you should at this point be able to help create a workable arrangement. It is your job to keep everyone calm, as the seating chart is very often a powder keg that detonates family fights and frustrates the already overloaded bride. As the process wears on, remind people to take their time, to know that it's not going to work out perfectly the first time, and that everyone will eventually find a seat.

Suggest frequent time-outs, break for dinner or drinks, and then get back to the job.

Seating Chart No-Nos

Don't Sit This Person . . .	With This Person . . .	Because . . .

Guest Seating Chart
(Round Tables)

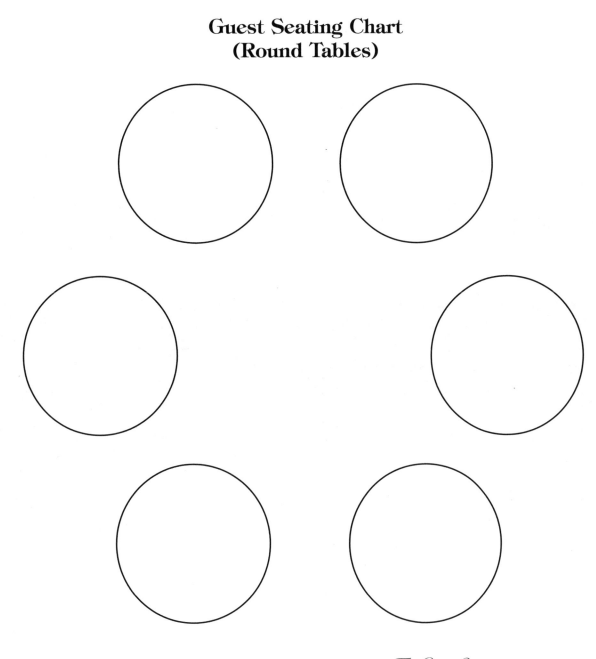

Guest Seating Chart
(Rectangular Tables)

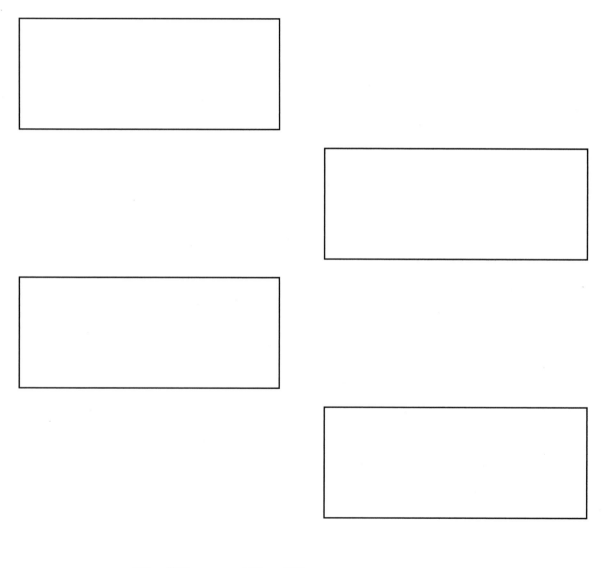

5

When and Where

YOU PROBABLY WON'T HAVE MUCH TO DO with this decision, but I've included it here because you may have some positive or negative input regarding the dates and places the bride and groom are considering. Perhaps you may have religious reasons for not wanting a particular wedding date, and you'd like to suggest that your daughter consider another day. Perhaps you've been to outdoor weddings during August, and you feel the heat may be too much for older relatives. You may believe your daughter hasn't taken valid points into consideration. It's *how* you bring about the suggestion that matters.

❧

I could tell my Mom was scared to remind me that the day I picked was a rather negative anniversary in the family. I was glad she said something, because I had completely forgotten. She was so nervous about coming to me with that!

—Shea, bride

❧

Just how should you bring up an objection? Time it right. Ask the bride when she has some time to talk. It's not the best idea to swoop down on her the next time you see her, because she may have other big issues on her mind. This whole process is exponentially hard on her. It's her big life change, not just her big party.

A recent mother of the bride warned me that you should keep in mind that the littlest thing could set the bride off. She may feel torn in twenty directions. Everyone is running to her with his or her requests (and not all of them as diplomatically as you are). She's had to change her plans so often that she may not even recognize the big day as hers anymore. How do you handle that? Give her a break. Take her out to coffee, but make it a no-wedding-talk time, which you should have every so often anyway.

☙

I had times when I hated it when anyone knocked on my bedroom door. I just knew it was someone else ready to change something I had planned. It just got so that I just wanted my way, *and that was final. My poor mom took the brunt of my stressed-out mood most often, and I see now that I was unfair to her.*

—Geri, bride

☙

Here's where you become the ambassador again. You respect your daughter's mood and wishes, but you just have to mention deer tick season to her. Catch her in a good mood and begin with "I know this is not what you want to agonize over right now, but I have a valid point I just wouldn't feel right about keeping from you. Since you haven't made your final decision about an outdoor wedding yet, I hope you'll think about this: That date is deer tick season." Short, sweet, and to the point. You haven't bossed her around (which she's probably extremely sensitive to), and you haven't ordered her to change the date. You've worded it so that you got your point across, she knows you're telling her that because you want her to know,

and she respects that you understand how difficult it all is on her now. Diplomacy is everything.

There are other date and time issues to keep in mind, as gentle reminders to the bride and groom. Be sure to bring these up at the beginning of the process. If the bride and groom pick and book a date, your knowledge of these issues will only frustrate them and cause them headaches over having to change it.

Things to Keep in Mind When Setting a Date

1. A holiday weekend does mean that people have an extra day to get to the wedding, but what will travel be like for them?
2. Religious holidays may mean that your guests cannot eat certain things at the reception.
3. Standard commercial holidays may mean elevated prices and lack of availability.
4. Too many hours between the ceremony and the reception may cause your guests to skip the ceremony and just attend the reception.
5. Avoid a sibling's birthday or graduation time. They're already hurting from the lack of attention.
6. Consider pregnant friends' or relatives' due dates. A pregnant bridesmaid may not want to be enormous during the wedding—or unable to attend due to early delivery.
7. Allow for enough time to plan the wedding well. A wedding set for three months from now will not provide the necessary time for booking, ordering, and comparison shopping.
8. Consider a sentimental date—such as the day the couple first met.
9. Don't enforce a sentimental date of your own—such as your wedding date.
10. June, August, and September are the big wedding months. Availability may be limited, and your guests may have other weddings to attend. Choose an off-season month, such as January through April, and availability will be increased.

11. Avoid the time of year that has your town hopping. Tourist season, conference season, or any special event that's going to be in town will book up all hotel rooms and raise prices. Check with your Chamber of Commerce on this.

12. Consider a Friday night wedding. This is a new, popular choice that is much less expensive than the Saturday wedding, and the couple saves further on honeymoon airline travel by being able to travel on a Saturday. No dragging themselves exhausted to an airport after the long wedding day and night.

Now what about the location? Keep in mind when you're all brainstorming for a wedding location those special places the couple holds dear—perhaps the spot of their first date. It's up to them to consider the site of your own wedding reception years ago. You can make an innocent plug, but don't put the pressure on. Sure, it would be nice, but it's their day. They may very well surprise you by already knowing that and wanting such a wonderful family connection.

Things to Keep in Mind When Considering Ceremony Locations

This may be a nonissue. The bride and groom may simply decide to have the ceremony at the church your family already attends. If that is the case, it is simply an issue of availability. Of course, the bride and groom may envision a completely different location, such as a beach, a hilltop, a garden, a gazebo, or even a lighthouse. This, again, is where you may have to suspend your judgment. It may be that you wouldn't dream of marrying anywhere but in the church, but it is not your wedding. Undoubtedly, the bride and groom—if they know you well—already know your feelings about a church or synagogue wedding, and they may hesitate to bring up the issue of their alternate plans. If they have chosen, say, the beach, your role is not to judge, but to assist. They may need you to help bring in the realities of booking such a site. You can remind them of important issues to consider.

1. The cost. Many parks, beaches, outdoor sites, historic homes, and so forth, require a permit or site fee. Check with the local Chamber of Commerce to find out what kinds of charges apply, what the application process is, and the availability. Please keep in mind that you must get permission from the town in order to have the wedding at a public place. You cannot just plan to set up your event without a permit, as the local police will most likely arrive to shut it down and arrest everyone for public drinking and noise violations.

2. The weather. If it rains, is there adequate shelter, or will you have to pack it in and run? An outdoor wedding means dealing with the elements, and in many ways this requires double planning. You will have to make sure there is an alternate site in case Mother Nature does not cooperate. Keep in mind that hot days mean sweaty guests, the possibility of heatstroke and sunburns, and a wedding cake that melts off its pedestal. Windy days may have the bride struggling with her flapping veil. A recent rain could have the ground too muddy to walk on.

3. Scheduling. Is the site booked tightly? Will you have to rush in at 1:00 and be out by 2:00 so that the next wedding can come in?

4. Accessibility. Can wheelchair-bound or elderly guests reach the wedding location with ease? It may be difficult to get a wheelchair through the forest path to that scenic waterfall. Elderly relatives may trip and hurt themselves.

5. Distance. Will you really feel like driving an hour to the wedding, then a distance to the reception? A beautiful site will be wonderful for the wedding pictures, but if it means requiring your guests to trek to the far ends of the earth, it may be better to choose a closer location. Consider also the threat of traffic, breakdowns, flat tires, lost guests, and accidents.

6. Appearance. Does the location have natural beauty? Be sure to look at it at the time of year that you will be holding the wedding. That flower-strewn hilltop may be gorgeous in spring, but after a long, dry summer you'll be crunching through dry grass.

7. Parking. Is there a nearby parking lot that can accommodate your guests? You don't want them to have to park six blocks away or leave the ceremony to pop

quarters into a meter. You may need to get a parking permit for large groups. Check with your Chamber of Commerce for rules and regulations to that effect.

8. Bathrooms. Inevitably, one or more of your guests will have a bathroom emergency. It may be the flower girl. It may be Uncle Ed. You don't want your guests to have to traipse into the woods for relief.

9. Electricity. The videographer, among others, may need power, so will the absence of electricity ruin the show?

10. Privacy. Will onlookers be free to wander through your private event? Teenagers and rowdy frat boys may find it hysterical to shout out obscenities and otherwise make a scene, and that kind of intrusion will be forever locked onto the wedding video. You may not be able to barricade strangers away, but keep in mind that a public place means the possibility of others around.

How to Deal With Criticism About the Ceremony Location

If the bride and groom have chosen an alternate location for the ceremony, no doubt someone will have a problem with forsaking religious locations. When Grandma or Aunt Bess starts squawking, your reply is that it's the kids' wedding, and they will have what they want. By no means should you approach the bride and groom to change their minds just to appease the Old World relatives. If the guests still object, they're free to skip the ceremony.

What if the bride and groom wish to have the ceremony at home? That is, *your* home. You may be overjoyed at the prospect, but this brings up certain issues for you. What kind of work does it entail for you? Will you have to have the place professionally cleaned? Carpet stains removed? Ceilings painted? Would you be too nervous about guests spilling bright red punch on your new beige carpeting? This is something you will have to think hard about. The kids are obviously pulled toward the sentimentality of having the ceremony in the bride's childhood home. She may have dreamed of coming down the stairs to the strains of "Here Comes the Bride." How can you say no? By having a mature conversation with the couple. If you truly feel that this option is not viable for you, you will have to make your wishes known in a diplomatic and noncontrolling way.

It is important for you to be honest with yourself here. Don't play the martyr and say yes if your heart says no. Discuss this option with your husband, and see if there is a possibility of this arrangement working out.

There are some logistics to think about, too. Where will the guests park? A permit will be needed. Will the neighbors care about the noise? Noise violations warrant tickets nowadays, and you don't want to have to close down the party at a too-early hour. You also don't want the neighbors disturbed. Where will you keep the dog during the party? Do you have to worry about a drain on the electricity? Will you have to worry about stocking the bathrooms with toilet paper every hour?

This may seem overdramatic, but other families of brides and grooms have pronounced this charming option a nightmare. Be sure you've considered all the elements before you decide to have an at-home wedding.

The worksheet on page 66 is to be used for coordinating locations. It may take a little bit of legwork to plan a ceremony time that leads into an available reception location. If you're called upon to do this research, here's your work space.

Location Worksheet

Ceremony Location _____

_____

Phone Number _____

Contact _____

Dates Available _____

_____

_____

Times Available _____

_____

_____

Location Notes (what's included, what's allowed, special rules) _____

_____

_____

_____

_____

Cost _____

Clip Brochure/Additional Notes Here

Choosing the Reception Location

This is a monumental job, and it will undoubtedly be up to the bride and groom themselves to scout out the locations for their reception. You may or may not be invited along for the initial comparison shopping jaunts, and, as long as they stay within the budget, it is up to the couple if they want you to take a look at the place before they sign any papers.

Wedding guidebooks do instruct the bride about the ins and outs of choosing a location, but I will provide for you here some of the things that brides forget to check for. Your job, then, is not to try to control the choice of banquet hall, but to make sure the bride and groom have thought of every possible factor.

1. Is it big enough? Make sure there is a definite head count before a site is booked. Never book a reception site with a guess as to how many guests will come. Assume all of the guests on the list will be there and book the site for that number. Make sure the banquet hall manager can assure you that the room is big enough for your wedding. If possible, arrange to see the room set up with the appropriate number of tables, so that you can see just how much room there is to move.

&

We were appalled to find that when we showed up for the reception, they had tables set up on the dance floor. When dinner was over, those guests had to leave their tables with drinks in hand. Three burly kitchen workers came out and hauled the tables away so that there was room for dancing.

—Talia, mother of the bride

&

2. How is the decor? Is it a neutral color that will look nice with the colors of the flowers and decorations? A garish, bright red room will look like a bordello. The bridesmaids' pink dresses will clash with the walls.

3. What about noise? Arrange to be in the room when there is an event going on next door so you can hear just how soundproof the dividing wall is.

4. How are the bathrooms? Check them for cleanliness and working utilities.

5. Is there a coatroom? You don't want guests sitting on their coats or getting strawberry sauce on the jackets that hang on the backs of their chairs.

6. What will the help be wearing? Make sure the waiters' wardrobe works with the formality of the wedding.

7. Is there adequate parking? Valet service?

8. How is the view? If there is a picture window, what does it look out upon?

9. Is it a fire trap? If the reception hall is downstairs, is there a fire exit?

10. Is it easily accessible? Your elderly or handicapped guests may not be able to make it up and down the stairs easily. If there is a spiral staircase, consider the burden on your guests.

11. Are there plenty of electrical outlets in the room for the DJ and videographer? Count them along each wall.

12. See the kitchen. Look for cleanliness, and yes, ask to see their inspection certificate.

13. Ask to taste the food if it is prepared on site.

14. Is there enough room for the band or DJ in front of the dance floor? You don't want the full band's equipment to take up half the dance floor.

15. Is the place clean? Check for floors that have not been vacuumed, burned-out lightbulbs, peeling paint, and so forth.

16. Are there places to take pictures? A garden out back, a gazebo, a pond, or a lake makes a good setting for portraits.

17. Is the banquet manager organized and willing to answer your questions? If he or she does not return calls, take that as a sign of lack of professionalism and move on.

18. Is liquor allowed? Some sites do not have a liquor license and may not allow you to bring in your own supply of champagne and liquors.
19. Is there a smoking area, such as an attached bar or smoking parlor? Your guests who smoke will not relish the idea of having to go outside for a cigarette. Are cigars allowed?
20. What is your gut feeling about the place? Can the bride see herself celebrating her marriage there?

Of course, other questions will come up, and the bride and groom may approach you with their concerns. If their mood is such that any questions from you will send them over the edge, just show them this list and allow them to consider the options on their own.

Use the comparison chart on page 70 while checking out reception sites.

Reception Worksheet

Reception Location _____

_____

Phone Number _____

Fax _____

E-mail _____

Contact _____

Dates Available _____

_____

Times Available _____

_____

☐ Adequate parking   ☐ Electrical outlets

☐ Valet service   ☐ Bathroom okay

☐ Separate cocktail area   ☐ Liquor allowed

☐ Appearance okay   ☐ Smoking area

☐ Big enough   ☐ Coat check

☐ Sound okay

Other Notes

Clip Brochure/Additional Notes Here

6

The Wedding Reception

THIS IS THE LARGEST AND MOST INVOLVED part of wedding planning. It's also the part that is most apparent to your guests, often the standard by which most weddings are judged. Before you start to worry about what everyone else will think, though, be reminded that this, too, is a major stumbling block between brides and their mothers. Some brides may want a simple, hors d'oeuvres-only cocktail hour while Mom wants nothing less than a nine-course ultraformal affair. Some moms—and it doesn't even matter whether they're paying for the wedding—feel that the reception is a reflection on *their* tastes and standards, not the bride's. You want the reception to reflect your good taste, but you must remind yourself that you ultimately want to give your daughter the wedding *she's* always dreamed of. So, if she wants cake and coffee only, so be it. She may not regret it for the rest of her life, as you fear. She would regret not having the reception she wanted, though.

On the following pages are worksheets for comparing all the professionals who will work to build this wonderful celebration. Since each element of the reception comes from some sort of wedding industry professional, a great deal of research, shopping around, sampling, and questioning is in order. This task can take months, but it is a necessary step in choosing the perfect pieces of the day. Knowing this, the bride—busy as she is with school or with work—may ask you to take over a little of the legwork in choosing some of the industry experts, or at least do the calling and researching so that she can make her decisions.

So here's where you take your notes when you're calling around town. Under each section, you'll find some of the most important questions to ask, covering all bases and avoiding the most common wedding nightmares, such as forgotten details and incomplete packages.

Keep in mind the good consumer rules we spoke of before, and always research several options. Never stop at the first one that sounds good. The more choices you sift through, the better your chances of discovering a gem.

The Caterer

Choosing a caterer is an enormous job. This is the person who will create and present the menu, and it is his or her quality of service and professionalism that will most be apparent to your guests. After all, the guests will remember if the food was heavenly, and they will remember if it was freezer-burned. They'll speak for months about the wonderful appetizers, the coconut shrimp, the mustard-glazed salmon. Your choice of caterer can make the difference between an unforgettable reception and a blemish on the whole day.

Where do you start? First, collect the names and phone numbers of local caterers. Here's how to get your list. Do not just open up the Yellow Pages and pick the caterer with the biggest ad. You'll best serve your daughter by brainstorming about the recent formal events you have attended. Think of weddings and bar or bat mitzvahs you've been to in the last year. Did you love the food? Did it make a lasting impression on you? Call the hosts or hostesses of those events and ask for their caterers' names and numbers. This is often the absolute best way to find and hire a quality caterer. If their services have been proven to you firsthand already, you have some degree of certainty that they will be able to fill your reception needs.

If you haven't been to a formal event in a long time, ask recently married friends or other recent mothers of brides if they can recommend a caterer. It is important for you to realize that in most wedding industry businesses, the majority of contacts are built on word of mouth and referrals. There are plenty of high-quality wedding experts, and they are the most recommended ones.

Of course, you can and should include some selections from the Yellow Pages in your starters list. Just be sure to subject them to the same kind of scrutiny you give all of your vendors. Test them on all levels.

Once you have your list of possibilities, call each for an initial consultation. Very often, you will speak to a clerk or receptionist, not the main caterer, and that person will take some specific information from you in order to assess if they indeed are the right caterer for you. You will need to supply the following:

1. The date of the wedding
2. The time of the wedding
3. The location of the wedding
4. If it is an outdoor or home wedding
5. The size of the wedding
6. What kind of reception it will be—formal dinner, hors d'oeuvres, and so forth

At this point, she will be able to tell you if the caterer is available to work for you on that day and if she can meet your needs. She will most likely either fax you a copy of her menu options and professional services contracts or invite you in for a sit-down consultation. Either of these options is fine, but you must know that the invitation for a sit-down chat is a sign of a caterer who is willing to listen to you, willing to show you samples or photographs of her work. It is a chance for you to meet her, see her work space, and get a general feel for her professional attitude. Since most of the client-customer relationship will be interpersonal, this is a sign that the caterer understands her role and wishes to make you comfortable in yours. So always go for the meet-and-greet.

At this meeting, you may be shown menus and lists of options. It is a smart use of your time to know what the bride and groom want and don't want as a part of the wedding menu. If your job at this time is just to collect preliminary info, limit your decision making. Be prepared to offer what the bride and groom have already expressed an interest in. By no means should you overstep the bride's decisions just because you have seen something wonderful on the menu that she hasn't thought of herself.

Ask for copies of the menus and package options, complete with prices and the inclusions of extras, and get copies of any other readily available wedding literature or brochures.

The General Rules for Hiring Caterers

1. Book them early. Make this one of the first decisions and hirings. The best caterers, remember, are widely recommended, and their plates—so to speak— may be full. I advise looking a full year in advance.
2. Ask for their professional credentials. Always hire a caterer who is state-certified and a member of a professional association.
3. Ask if they have liability insurance. If not, you could be sued for your guests' food poisoning. It has happened.
4. Ask how long they have been in business. While a new start-up may be outstanding, complete with the full recommendation of a quality culinary institute, you may wish to hire someone who has years of experience and a good flow to her techniques.

Warning!

Do not be too quick to hire other wedding professionals through the caterer's recommendation. You may be offered seemingly good discounts for hiring the caterer's photographer friend, but these kinds of piggyback deals rarely work out for the best. Take each entry as an individual entity. You may choose to include this particular photographer in your list, and if he turns out to be the best of the bunch, you can then take the discount.

Questions to Ask a Catering Company

These are the questions that you should ask as you assess any particular caterer's suitability for your wedding needs. You can then use this information to fill in the caterer comparison chart on pages 78–79.

1. How many weddings have you done?
2. Have you catered a wedding this size before?
3. Can you provide me with references from your other clients?
4. What are some of the wedding menu themes that you have done?
5. Do you have photos of other wedding spreads that you have created?
6. Are menu tastings available?
7. Do you require guests to specify their entrée selections in advance?
8. Do you offer vegetarian menu choices?
9. Do you offer the kinds of ethnic foods that we'd like?
10. Do you have a kosher menu?
11. How many hors d'oeuvres do you supply per guest?
12. How many different packages do you have?
13. Am I free to custom design a package?
14. What are your rental fees for linens and flatware, and so forth?
15. Am I free to hire my own rentals, or do you require us to go through you for those services?
16. How many other events do you have to do that week or weekend?
17. If there are no other events booked that weekend right now, how close are you likely to book any parties you get in the future?
18. Which of your entrée and appetizer specialties have received the most raves from your other clients?
19. What are your refund or cancellation policies and fees?
20. Who will do the serving?
21. How many waiters will you provide?
22. What will the waiters wear?
23. How experienced are the waiters?
24. What happens if the guest count decreases before the event? Will we still have to pay what is agreed upon at the outset, or are you flexible until the last minute?
25. Can we provide additional dishes or desserts?
26. Where do you prepare the food, if not on site?
27. Can I look at your kitchen?

28. Has the kitchen passed inspection?
29. Are you familiar with the site we have selected?
30. What kind of discounts can you offer us?
31. What is the serving schedule—i.e., how many hours pass between dinner and dessert?
32. Where do you get your liquor from? Can we provide our own?
33. Will you, the caterer, be present on the wedding day to answer questions and solve problems?
34. What other services do you provide?
35. What are your hidden fees?

During this question and answer period you will likely learn a great deal about the caterer's abilities to serve you well. You will also learn how willing she is to accommodate you. If the caterer you're interviewing seems bored or just says, "It's all in our literature here," then move on. This person is not the right choice. A quality professional will know that you are simply asking responsible questions in order to hire the best caterer.

Use the comparison sheet template on pages 78–79 for your final analysis of each caterer. Then present this information, along with all pertinent menus and other papers, to the bride and groom for their review.

As with any good business relationship, you will want to make sure you have a solid contract drawn up with the caterer of your choice. This contract is the entire business agreement between you, and it will protect your investment only if it is a complete document that covers all of the issues you have discussed with the caterer.

So when you're ready to sign on the dotted line, if it has been assigned to you to do so, make sure the following information is in the contract. If your daughter and her fiancé will be doing this, make sure they have this list with them.

To be Included in the Caterer's Contract

- The bride's and groom's name
- The date of the wedding

- Backup date (if applicable)
- The time of the wedding
- The exact location of the wedding, including street address and phone number
- The name of the catering company
- The name of the caterer who will be working your event
- The guest count
- Specific notes about being flexible with head count until a set date before the wedding
- The menu package or selections made
- Rental agreements, with specific numbers of specific items
- What is not the caterer's responsibility
- The caterer's agreement to attend the event
- Number of servers
- What the servers will wear
- Liquor agreement
- Passed hors d'oeuvres agreement
- Buffet or dinner times
- Decor to be provided by the caterer
- Costs, including any extras
- Deposit schedule
- Refund or cancellation fees and requirements
- Gratuity agreement
- "Time is of the Essence" clause, which states that the vendor agrees to deliver her products and services by a certain time, or she is in violation of the contract

Know that you should always read every word of the contract, ask questions about what you do not understand, cross off what you don't want, and initial any changes. If a caterer is unwilling to let you change *any* wording in the contract, move on. You should always be given your own copy of the contract. Again, if not, move on.

Caterer Worksheet

Name of Caterer _____

Contact Person _____

Address _____

Phone _____

Fax _____

E-mail _____

Package Name and Elements _____

_____

☐ Or see attached brochure/menus

☐ Professional membership

☐ Years of experience

☐ Insured

☐ Willing to customize menu

☐ Provides extras

☐ Will be present on wedding day

☐ Offers tastings

Tasting Notes _____

_____

☐ Willing to listen, patient, responds quickly

☐ Recommended by

Cost _____

☐ Deposit fee

☐ Deposit payment schedule

☐ Itemized contract offered

☐ Refund policy

☐ Cancellation policy

Notes (include time, date, and with whom you spoke) _____

_____

_____

_____

_____

_____

_____

Attach Brochure Here

Wedding-Cake Baker

If you won't be getting the wedding cake from the caterer—and you should always check out other vendors for better pricing, design, and custom options—you'll need to comparison shop among bakeries and wedding-cake specialists. Again, get referrals from recently married friends or, for proven reliability, use your family's regular bakery.

When checking out a baker's suitability, ask the following questions:

1. How many years of experience do you have?
2. How many wedding cakes have you done?
3. Can I see pictures of cakes you've done?
4. What kinds of cake, filling, and icing options do you offer?
5. What kinds of designs do you offer?
6. What kinds of topping or garnishes do you offer?
7. Do you deliver?
8. What is your delivery fee?
9. What is your refund/cancellation policy?
10. Can we taste samples of your work?

A good baker will let you sample pieces of cake, and he or she will let you design what you want. You will need to let the baker know about the wedding's formality, location, and the wishes of the bride and groom. Again, do not take it upon yourself to make this decision. You may not know that the groom is allergic to strawberries, so even if the harried bride tells you to book what you want, always double-check the options with her.

One thing to keep in mind, and it is the thing that is most often forgotten: If the wedding will be held outdoors, get a buttercream frosting. It holds up better in warm weather. Also, if flowers are to be used as garnish for the cake, double-check with a florist to be sure the flowers you choose are not toxic. And if a customized cake topper will be used on top of the cake, get it weighed precisely so the baker can be sure the cake's top layer is big enough and strong enough to hold it.

Use the bakery comparison sheet on page 81 to compare wedding-cake bakers.

Wedding Cake Worksheet

Bakery _____

Contact Name _____

Address _____

Phone Number _____

Fax _____

E-mail _____

Cake Chosen _____

☐ Topper included?

☐ Floral garnish?

☐ Delivery fee?

☐ Refund/cancellation fees? _____

☐ Tastings available?

Notes _____

_____

_____

Attach Brochure Here

Entertainment

This is another area of utmost importance to the quality of the reception. A good DJ or band will make the evening enjoyable, but only if the right choice is made for professionalism, talent, and suitability to your crowd.

If you have been asked to help out in this area, then keep in mind some of the issues involved.

Do You Want a DJ or a Band?

This is the main decision, the first hurdle to leap. Obviously, a good DJ can provide many more types of songs than can be performed by a band. Some people prefer to hear the original, quality recordings of their favorite numbers, and some people prefer live music. Ask the bride and groom if they have a specific choice in mind. Again, remove yourself from the decision. You may think it would be unwise to have a DJ set up in the corner of the room, but the kids may have no problem with it.

Remind the bride and groom that having a band usually means that you'll have to feed the members of the band, and those spaces take up valuable room on the guest list. Do you want to feed twelve musicians, or twelve of your daughter's college friends?

Finding the Options

Again, start by asking the recently married whom they hired. Ask for referrals. Before you start searching, have an idea of what kinds of music the bride and groom want played at the wedding. Perhaps they want a wide range of songs from the 1940s to current-day hits. Perhaps, if it is a theme wedding, they'll want only music that fits the theme. Or maybe they simply want a classic music quintet to play softly in the background. Only by knowing what the bride and groom want can you begin to sift through the options.

Questions to Ask DJs

1. How long have you been doing this?
2. Are you a staff member of a DJ company, or are you in business for yourself?

3. Do you have other clients I can contact for a review of your work?
4. Do you have a videotape of yourself in action?
5. Can we come see you live at another function?
6. Do you have a song catalog that I can review?
7. Do you have, or can you get, the bride's and groom's requests for specific songs?
8. What will you wear to the wedding?
9. What kind of audience participation things do you do?
10. How many hours will you work?
11. What are your overtime fees?
12. How many breaks do you take?
13. Do you play music during your breaks?
14. Do you act as the emcee for the evening?
15. What are your cancellation/refund fees?
16. Do you offer a standard contract?

Questions to Ask a Band

1. How long have you been performing together?
2. How many weddings have you done?
3. Can I see a video of your performance?
4. Can I see you perform live at another function?
5. How many hours do you work?
6. How many breaks do you take?
7. Does someone provide music when the rest of the band takes a break?
8. What is your song catalog, and can I see a copy?
9. Will you be willing to learn any special-request songs the bride and groom want?
10. Will we be informed if your band changes members ahead of time?
11. Will you act as the emcee for the evening?
12. Can you perform ethnic songs that we want?
13. What will you wear for the event?
14. What are your fees?
15. What are your overtime fees?
16. What is your refund/cancellation fee?
17. Do you offer a standard contract?

Band and DJ Worksheet

Name of Band or DJ ....

Contact Name ....

Address ....

Phone Number ....

Fax ....

E-mail or Web site ....

☐ Years of experience _____   ☐ Cost ....

☐ Referrals offered   ☐ Overtime fees ....

☐ Offers song list   ☐ Cancellation/refund policy

☐ Willing to buy/learn new songs   ☐ Offers contract

☐ Willing to provide video of performance   ☐ Wardrobe okay

☐ Willing to allow live preview   ☐ Emcees

☐ Willing to audition   ☐ Hours worked ....

Notes ....

....

Attach Brochure Here

Photographer

If the bride has asked you to help choose a photographer, you know by now that this will take some comparison shopping. Again, start by asking relatives and friends for referrals. Don't forget to ask your corporate clients if they know of a good photographer. Very often, corporations hire the best photographers to shoot their grounds and headquarters for important brochures, press kits, and stockholders' meetings. This is an excellent way to get a good referral.

You will most likely find the best photographer through a recently married friend or mother of the bride. Through that person, you will be able to look at an actual wedding album to check for quality of product and range of pictures. Your friend can tell you what was good or bad about the photographer, and you can base your decision from there. Again, the best wedding photographers in the area go by word of mouth, and the best quality choices are in high demand. So start looking early.

Ask to come in to see samples of the photographer's work. A true professional will have plenty of options to show you. What you are looking for is a wide range of shots, those that make use of natural lighting and the beauty of the settings. The best wedding photos go beyond the standard in-studio portrait to capture the feeling of the day itself.

As you review sample photos, you will also be handed a listing of the photographer's package deals. Very often, these range from simple, low-cost basic packages to all-out, high-expense packages. It is up to the bride and groom to decide what kind of photos they want, how many albums they need, and what kinds of special effects shots they require. Your job is to collect the data, find out all pertinent information, and report back to them.

Questions to Ask a Photographer

1. How long have you been in business?
2. How many weddings have you done?
3. How many other weddings do you have to do that month?

4. Are you available all day on that date, or will you have to leave at a certain time?
5. What are your package fees?
6. What are your optional extras?
7. Do you charge less for black and white pictures?
8. Can I custom design a package?
9. Do we get to keep the proofs?
10. How long does it take for delivery?
11. Do you offer a standard contract?
12. What are your refund/cancellation policies and fees?
13. What will you wear to the wedding?
14. What kind of equipment do you use?
15. Is it in good, working order?
16. Do you bring spare cameras to the event in case of a problem?
17. How many rolls of film do you shoot?
18. Do you develop the film yourself, or do you send it out?
19. Do you offer retouching?
20. Do you offer special lenses and film for special-effects shots?
21. What are your available enlargement sizes?
22. What kinds of wedding album designs do you offer?
23. What do you charge for thank-you note pictures and picture holders?
24. Are you insured?
25. How many hours do you work?
26. What are your overtime fees?

A good photographer will take the time to explain all you need to know about what he does. He will be willing to answer all of your questions and show you as many different kinds of pictures that you wish to see. He'll be willing to customize packages for you, and he'll be willing to customize the contract for you.

Photographer Worksheet

Photographer Studio _____

Contact Name _____

Address _____

Phone Number _____

Fax _____

E-mail _____

Package Name _____

☐ Wide range of packages

☐ Quality equipment

☐ Number of rolls of film used

☐ Offers black and white shots

☐ Offers special-effects shots

☐ Allows us to keep the proofs

☐ Wardrobe okay

☐ Delivery time

☐ Special requests granted

☐ Cost

☐ Overtime

☐ Deposit schedule

☐ Offers written contract

Notes _____

_____

Attach Brochure Here

To be Included in Photographer's Contract

- Name of the bride and groom
- Wedding date
- Time of wedding
- Time that photographer should show up at bride's home
- Address and phone number of bride's home
- Exact ceremony location, with street address
- Time that photographer should show up at ceremony location
- Exact list of shots to be taken at the ceremony
- Post-ceremony location, with street address and times
- Time of reception
- Location of reception, with street address
- Hours of reception work
- List of shots to get
- Overtime fees
- Wardrobe requirements (tuxedo, etc.)
- Delivery date
- Permission to keep proofs
- Album order
- Special-effects shots
- Refund/cancellation policy
- Payment schedule, including deposits
- Signature of photographer to work that day

Videographer

The videographer is going to capture the day for posterity. In order to hire the best videographer, you need to know something about video itself. Photographs are relatively easy to figure out: You need only to know about sizes and color and black and white. With video, it's much more involved. So here is where you'll learn about what goes into making a truly top-quality wedding videotape.

According to Steve Blahitka of Back East Productions in East Hanover, New Jersey, the process starts with finding out what kind of equipment the videographer uses, and what kind of film stock he'll use. We'll take these one at a time. A 3-chip camera is better than a 1-chip camera; 3-chip produces a better image.

It doesn't end there. The kind of film stock the videographer will use with his camera also matters. You can get a good video with a high-quality camera and a lesser quality film stock, and you can also get a good product with a lower quality camera and a high-quality film stock. Huh?

The best tape formats are digital and beta. VHS and Hi-8 are of slightly lesser quality, but they will still make a top-quality picture if used with the 3-chip camera. For a wedding video of top quality, you should ask for a 3-chip camera and any of the four top film stocks: digital, beta, VHS, and Hi-8.

The videographer should be able to explain what kinds of cameras and stock he uses, but if you aren't aware of the classification, that information will be useless to you. So you should know some of this terminology and have a basic understanding that the quality of film stock is going to affect the quality of the wedding video picture. So go for the high end of both. It will cost more, but in the end, the product is worth it.

You might be tempted to get one master copy and make duplicates yourself on your own VCR. I would advise against this, because any copying you do on your own can produce less-than-perfect copies, and it could damage your master. So have the videographer produce the exact number of videotapes you want duplicated.

A good videographer will have professional quality lighting and sound equipment. Most videographers have clip-on microphones that they put on the groom's lapel before the service. This is the best way to get a good recording of the vows and wording of the ceremony. Be sure the videographer can accommodate this request.

One thing you should watch out for is a special-effects junkie. Some videographers think that adding tons of special effects and titles makes for a better wedding video, but the result very often ends up looking garish and distracting. A certain amount of special framing is good, but all things should be in moderation, and the effects should be suitable for the formality of the wedding. One bride told me that there were digital tennis players running through the frame during her first dance with her husband. Neither of them plays tennis. And the Easter bunny hopped through the footage of the best man's toast. The wedding was in December. So don't allow the videographer to go nuts with the effects.

Questions to Ask the Videographer

1. How long have you been doing this?
2. How many weddings have you done?
3. Do you belong to a professional association?
4. What kind of camera do you use?
5. What kind of film stock do you use?
6. Do you bring a spare camera to the event?
7. How much footage will you shoot?
8. What kind of lighting do you have?
9. What kind of microphones do you have?
10. How long will it take for you to edit the video?
11. How long until we can expect delivery?
12. What kinds of video packages do you offer?
13. Can we customize the package?
14. What do you charge for duplication?
15. Do you label the videos?
16. Can I see the label designs you offer?
17. Do you provide videotape jackets?
18. What kinds of titles or special effects do you do?
19. How many hours do you work?
20. What are your overtime fees?
21. Do you offer a refund/cancellation policy?
22. Do you offer a written contract?
23. What is your payment/deposit schedule?
24. What do you plan to wear to the wedding?

Items to be Included in Videographer's Contract

- Name of the bride and groom
- Wedding date and time
- Location of the bride's home, including street address, for pre-wedding footage
- Groom's location, including street address, for pre-wedding footage
- Hours of pre-wedding work
- Location of the ceremony, including street address
- Time of the ceremony
- Post-ceremony locations and times
- Reception location and times
- Specification of equipment and film stock
- Hours of footage agreed upon
- Package agreed upon
- Payment schedule
- Deposit schedule
- Refund/cancellation fees
- Extra fees
- Duplicates
- Labels
- Jackets
- Event wardrobe
- Gratuities

Optional Footage

For a complete video package, you might consider having the videographer shoot some events other than those simply of the wedding day. Try having him attend—or agree to edit into the final package your own home footage from—the following events.

- The engagement party
- Bride and groom registering for gifts
- Bride shopping for her gown
- Band auditions (this can be *hysterical!*)
- Interviews with bride, groom, and family throughout the process
- Getting blood tests and the marriage license
- Wedding showers
- Bachelor's party and bachelorette's party
- Rehearsal
- Rehearsal dinner
- Bride and bridal party at salon on wedding morning
- Wedding morning interviews
- Groom getting ready
- Bridal brunch
- Post-wedding interviews

It is a very good idea to inform your photographer and videographer of any special shots you want taken. Perhaps the bride has a special great uncle, and you want to be sure there is footage of him dancing with her. Remember that your daughter is going to be in her own state of euphoria that day, so it is your job to make sure all of those once-in-a-lifetime pictures are taken.

Just inform the videographer and photographer of your wishes for special shots to be taken, and they will understand when you keep showing up behind them to point their lenses in the right direction. A professional will understand your excitement, and he will not take offense at your telling him how to do his job.

Your daughter and her husband will thank you later.

Videographer Worksheet

Videography Studio _____

Contact Name _____

Address _____

Phone Number _____

Fax _____

E-mail _____

Package Name _____

☐ Wide range of packages   ☐ Special requests granted

☐ Quality equipment   ☐ Cost _____

☐ Hours of videotape footage available   ☐ Overtime _____

☐ Extra special effects   ☐ Deposit schedule _____

☐ Wardrobe okay   ☐ Offers written contract

☐ Delivery time _____   ☐ Cancellation/refund policy

Notes _____

_____

Attach Brochure Here

The Florist

Here is where the bride could use your help. She, of course, will want to choose the design of her bouquet herself, but you can save her a lot of time by doing the legwork to find the best florist for the job.

You may decide to use your family's regular florist, as they have proven their reliability to you. You may even know the owner by now, in which case you might get a discount for your wedding order. If you are stumped on which florist to use, again, get a referral from a recently married friend or relative.

When choosing a florist, it will usually be price that affects your decision. After all, a rose is a rose, and a wide variety of arrangements can be made for your design needs. Money will probably be the biggest factor, but there are smaller issues that need to be addressed.

Questions to Ask a Florist

1. How long have you been in business?
2. How many weddings have you done?
3. Have you done weddings of this size before?
4. Are you affiliated with a professional organization?
5. Are you state-licensed?
6. Can we speak to any of your former wedding clients for their referrals?
7. Can we see pictures of your work?
8. Can we stop in at a wedding to see live samples of your work?
9. What are your package rates?
10. What is included in your packages?
11. Do you deliver?
12. What is your delivery fee?
13. Do you offer any extras, such as aisle runners, chuppahs, and so forth?
14. What is your refund/cancellation fee?
15. Do you offer a written contract?
16. How many other weddings are you doing that weekend?

Your needs will most likely be similar to those of most weddings. As you interview florists, you should be able to provide information to enable them to assess your needs and whether or not they can meet them. These are:

1. The date of the wedding
2. The location of the wedding
3. The number of people in the bridal party
4. The number of guests who will receive corsages or boutonnieres
5. The number of centerpieces you will need
6. Any ceremony site decor
7. Any reception site decor

Of course, the florist will know that at this stage you haven't hammered out your plans yet, so all of this information is just to obtain a general ballpark figure.

At this time, you should also check out the florist's professionalism. What is the shop like? Is it clean? Are the flowers presented in an attractive manner? Are people rushing around, trying to complete an order? Is there an air of chaos about the place? Are the phones ringing off the hook? This is a good way to see if the place is overwhelmed. You can also tell by the way the salespeople treat customers who call just how well you will be treated when you have a question about your order.

Remember, it is the bride and groom who will make the actual decisions about the design of the bouquets and boutonnieres, but you can assist by making sure the bride and groom are aware of exactly what they need to order. They may not remember about the grandmothers' corsages, and they may not remember to order the floral wreath for the flower girl's hair. Again, this is not the time to step in and start giving orders. You might just mention to the bride that you have a chart, on pages 96–97, here for her use, which can save you from having to be a nag by reminding the bride of the often-forgotten floral orders.

Use the comparison sheet on page 98 to figure out which florist works best for you.

Floral Shopping List

Item	Number Needed	Price
Bride's bouquet		
Bride's throwaway bouquet		
Bridesmaids' bouquets		
Ushers' boutonnieres		
Groom's boutonniere		
Mother of the bride's corsage		
Father of the bride's boutonniere		
Grandmothers' corsages		
Grandfathers' boutonnieres		
Mother of the groom's corsage		
Father of the groom's boutonniere		
Grandmothers' corsages		
Grandfathers' boutonnieres		
Godparents' corsages		
Godparents' boutonnieres		
Flower girls' floral baskets		
Flower girls' floral wreaths		

Item	Number Needed	Price
Centerpieces		
Ceremony site decor		
Pew bows and floral pieces		
Aisle runner		
Unity candle		
Chuppah		
Reception decor		
Centerpieces		
Outdoor floral arrangements		
Trellises		
Floral elements for favors		
Rose petals for tossing		
Cake cutter		
Cake server		

Florist Worksheet

Florist Name _____

Contact Person _____

Address _____

Phone Number _____

Fax _____

E-mail _____

☐　State license

☐　Professional association

☐　Extensive catalogs

☐　Live designs to review

☐　Customized package

☐　Delivery

☐　Delivery fee _____

☐　Extras included

☐　Cost _____

☐　Deposit schedule _____

☐　Refund/cancellation policy

Notes _____

_____

Attach Brochure Here

To be Included in Florist's Contract

1. Name of bride and groom
2. Wedding date and time
3. Location of ceremony, with street address
4. Location of reception, with street address
5. Exact floral order, *itemized*
6. Delivery instructions
7. Payment schedule
8. "Time is of the essence" clause
9. Refund/cancellation policy
10. Gratuities
12. Set-up instructions

Delivery Instructions for Florist

Use the chart below to be sure your florist knows when and where certain items are to be delivered.

TO GO TO THE BRIDE'S HOME
Address:
Time:
Items:

TO GO TO THE RECEPTION LOCATION
Address:
Time:
Items:

TO GO TO THE GROOM'S LOCATION
Address:
Time:
Items:

TO GO TO OTHER LOCATIONS
Address:
Time:
Items:

TO GO TO THE CEREMONY LOCATION
Address:
Time:
Items:

❧

The florist brought the corsages and boutonnieres to the reception hall and not the church. So we had to pull roses out of our bouquets for the men's lapels.

—Tracy, bride

❧

Limousine Services

Here is another area where you can save the bride a lot of time by doing the calling, researching, and questioning yourself. You may choose to use a limousine company that your family, or your company, uses regularly.

When hiring for a wedding, though, it is more complex than arranging for a pickup or drop-off at the airport. You must take into account scheduling, various locations, time to wait, and extras to stock for the limo. Limousine companies are prepared for this. In most cases, just let them know what you need and when you need it, and they do the rest.

Questions to Ask a Limousine Company

1. How long have you been in business?
2. Are you state-certified?
3. How many cars are in your fleet?
4. How old are the cars?
5. Do you have a selection of colors?
6. Are the cars inspected?
7. Do you also rent Rolls Royces or other luxury cars?
8. Does the driver know this area?
9. What are your fees?
10. What are overtime fees?
11. Can we customize for pickups and drop-offs?

12. Do you stock champagne in the limo?
13. What about snacks?
14. What are your champagne and snack fees?
15. What do your drivers wear?
16. Do you have backup cars in case of a breakdown?
17. Do your drivers have cell phones?
18. Will the cars be cleaned and polished before the wedding day?
19. Are your drivers state-licensed?

Always make sure you are shown the actual cars that will be used on the wedding day. Some companies will show you their newest model, but then send an older one for your event if a higher profile client comes along in the meantime. So contract for the exact cars you want.

Make sure the cars are clean and fresh-smelling inside, and make sure the seats are without rips and tears. Some luxury limousines have full bars, ice, and minibars inside, so be sure you get your money's worth.

Limousine Pickup/Drop-off Schedule

LIMO NUMBER _____

Who Will be Picked Up: _____

Pickup Location: _____

Pickup Time: _____

Drop-off Location: _____

Drop-off Time: _____

LIMO NUMBER _____

Who Will be Picked Up: _____

Pickup Location: _____

Pickup Time: _____

Drop-off Location: _____

Drop-off Time: _____

Remember to Book Limousines (or Arrange Transportation) for:

1. Bride and parents to the ceremony site
2. Groom and parents to the ceremony site
3. Bridal party to the ceremony site
4. Other important family members to the ceremony site
5. Bride and groom to reception site
6. Bridal party to reception site
7. Bride's and groom's parents to reception site
8. Other family members to reception site
9. Bride and groom to accommodations site
10. Bridal party to homes
11. Bride's and groom's parents to homes
12. Other family members to homes

Don't forget about picking up and dropping off out-of-town relatives and friends at the airport. You may choose to have a limo get them, or you can arrange to use their hotel's free shuttle. Many airports have free phone lines to the major hotels in the area that they can use to arrange for a ride. Check if this option is available, and tell your guests to use it. This is a free service—and a big relief to you and your husband.

On page 103 is a worksheet for comparing limousine companies.

Limousine Worksheet

Limousine Company _____

Contact Name _____

Address _____

Phone Number _____

Fax _____

E-mail or Web site _____

☐ State certified

☐ Professional association

☐ Number of cars

☐ Appearance of cars

☐ Interior of cars

☐ Drivers licensed

☐ Drivers wardrobe okay

☐ Champagne and snacks

☐ Cost _____

☐ Payment schedule

☐ Refund or cancellation policy

☐ Offers written contract

Notes _____

_____

Attach Brochure Here

To Be Included in Limousine Company's Contract

- Bride's and groom's names
- Date and time of wedding
- Style of cars
- Number of cars
- Inspection guarantee
- Cleaning guarantee
- Exact pickup and drop-off schedule
- Driver's wardrobe
- Champagne and snacks to be stocked
- Guarantee of replacement car in case of breakdown
- Payment schedule
- Refund/cancellation fee
- Gratuities

7

The Engagement Party

THINK OF THIS AS your little mini-wedding to plan. Traditionally, the bride's parents host the first wedding celebration event, so the ball is in your court to plan a wonderful cocktail, dinner, or dessert party to honor the impending nuptials. Of course, it is also possible that you might choose to cohost this party with the groom's parents. Whatever your hosting decision, this is your time to plan a festive evening for the kids.

❧

My parents gave us a wonderful engagement party, complete with a pianist providing the music, waiters walking around with silver trays of coconut shrimp and bacon-wrapped scallops, and the most wonderful chocolate ganache cake. It was an elegant and exciting start to this whole chapter in our lives.

—Shea, bride

❧

Your party doesn't have to be a strolling violinist–type affair. It may just be a gathering of the immediate family and bridal party for the first time, a lovely dinner out, or even a home-cooked meal with excited conversation about the task at hand. This is your chance to kick off the festivities, to make this an enjoyable process right from the start.

The first thing you'll need to know is the actual wedding guest list, or the closest approximation of it you can get. It would be a mistake for you to invite three hundred relatives, friends, neighbors, and coworkers to this event, as it is an unwritten rule that those who are invited to the engagement party are also invited to the wedding. It would be rude to leave them out at a later date. Most parents of brides, in finding that the guest list is not complete, opt to host a simpler gathering of immediate family, close friends, the bridal party, and several others. They consider this an informal affair, to be shared by the bride's and groom's closest loved ones. So if the guest list is not yet complete, you can make your list of definites by including grandparents, siblings, close uncles and aunts, close cousins, the bridal party, the bride's and groom's best friends, and a few other chosen people.

An engagement party is never more formal than the wedding will be. Most engagement parties fall under the category of semiformal. Guests will wear dresses and suits to the dinner, which may be held at a nice restaurant or even at your home. An informal dinner may also be had at a family style restaurant or at your home. Brunches work well for engagement parties, as the variety of foods offered at a lavish brunch buffet differs from the kind of meals you'll likely enjoy at showers, the rehearsal, and the wedding itself. Don't rule out the comfy, informal barbecue, either.

Chances are, you already have a vision of what you want the engagement party to be like. You may be thinking of a catered lunch at a small banquet hall room or a catered cocktail hour in your home. Whatever your choice, you have some work to do as you make the general plans. First, you'll have to choose a caterer. We've already covered the basics of choosing a caterer in the reception chapter, so look back at those notes to assess your choices.

When you do find a caterer, think about the kind of menu you'd like to offer to your guests. Keep in mind the basics of forming the right menu for your event.

- It must fit the formality of the event.
- It must include foods that are in season.
- It must offer a wide variety of foods to suit the tastes of your guests.
- It must include items that adhere to your guests' dietary rules, such as vegetarian or kosher.
- The bride and groom must approve of your choices.

You may decide to skip the caterer and make the foods yourself. Many mothers of brides choose this option, preparing and sharing their world-famous recipes and family favorites. The bride and groom may want this as well, loving as they do your beef wellington or lobster bisque recipe. In a way, it adds a sense of family to the event; this might be a nice time to present the bride with her very own copies of the recipes that have been handed down to you by your mother and grandmother.

Whatever your arrangement, you'll need to consider menu options. I've divided the engagement party menus into the most basic categories, and I've listed some options for you to consider for inclusion in your event. Of course, your caterer, if you have one, will have his or her own menu, but this might give you an idea of the options that are available to you.

Engagement Party Menus

Brunch (10 A.M.–1 P.M.)

Juices—orange, grapefruit, tomato, apple
Coffees—regular, gourmet, flavored
Teas—regular, herbal
Mimosas—champagne mixed with orange juice
Fruits or fruit salads—include exotic fruits such as kiwi, starfruit, pineapple
Breads—muffins, croissants, pumpernickel, scones, and so forth
Bagels with a selection of flavored spreads
Waffles with a selection of fruit sauce toppings

Blintzes

Meats—bacon, sausage, taylor ham, Canadian bacon

Potatoes—hash browns, vegetable/potato mixes

Hot or cold cereals

Selection of pastries for dessert—napoleans, fruit tarts, chantilly cream tarts, eclairs, and so forth

Luncheons (11 A.M.–3 P.M.)

Cold cheese platter

Cold pepperoni and luncheon meats platter

Sandwiches—selection of tuna, "sloppy joes," cucumber, pastrami, and submarine sandwiches

Soups—seafood bisques, tomato, potato, bean and pasta, and so forth

Carving station foods—ham, beef, pork, turkey

Pastas—Pasta and vegetable mixes with a selection of marinara, alfredo, and pesto sauces

Breads—onion, foccaccia, French, garlic, and so forth

Selection of dessert pastries

Cheesecakes, chocolate mousse, white chocolate mousse, pies, petit fours, and so forth

Barbecues (11 A.M.–2 P.M.)

Selection of soft drinks

Selection of liquors

Meats—steaks, ribs, chicken pieces, burgers

Vegetables for grilling—portobello mushrooms, zucchini strips, peppers

Salads—green, potato, macaroni, pasta

Seafood—steamed crabs, crab legs, shrimp, lobster tails

Selection of pastries, brownies, or cookies for dessert

Fruit salads, fresh fruits

Teas (2 P.M.–4 P.M.)

Selection of herbal and regular teas
Selection of flavored, gourmet, and regular coffees
Selection of juices
Selection of breads—croissants, mini-rolls, and so forth
Finger sandwiches
Selection of cookies and pastries for dessert

Cocktail Parties (4 P.M.–7 P.M.)

Punches and soft drinks
Selection of liquors—wines, champagne, hard liquors
Cold cheese platter
Cold luncheon meat platter
Hors d'oeuvres—bacon-wrapped scallops, shrimp cocktail, sushi, pastry puff
   appetizers, and so on
Hot buffet items—lemon chicken, pastas, beef wellington
Selection of breads
Selection of pastries, pies, cheesecakes, mousses, cakes for dessert

Dinners (6 P.M.–9 P.M.)

Punches and soft drinks
Selection of liquors and champagnes
Salads—mesclun, arugala, Caesar
Selection of breads
Pastas—manicotti, stuffed shells, lasagna, penne with vegetables
Meats—prime rib, pork chops, turkey breast, meatballs
Selection of pastries, cheesecakes, pies, cakes, mousses for dessert

Desserts (8 P.M.–10 P.M.)

Selection of coffees, including espresso, cappuccino, Irish coffee
Selection of teas
After-dinner drinks—brandy, cognac, and so forth
Wide selection of cakes, pies, mousses, cheesecakes, fruit tarts, pastries

Decor

Decorating a banquet hall room is probably not necessary. Chances are a buffet table will have garnishes of its own. You might request some floral arrangements for the tables or even an ice sculpture.

If you are having the event at home, you might just spruce up the place a little. The simple placement of lavish floral arrangements around your home can add a festive touch to the atmosphere. One floral piece at the center of your serving table is fine, and you might choose to incorporate the bride's and groom's wedding colors into the arrangement.

For other decorating ideas, think about what these mothers of brides did for their daughters' engagement party decor.

We set a special table out by the door for the display of all of our family's wedding pictures, from Great-grandma on down to the engagement photo of the couple.

—Joanne, mother of the bride

We used flowers from my own garden, and placed them in tiny bud vases all around the house.

—Sylvia, mother of the bride

We had an angel theme at the engagement party, so we used most of our angel-oriented Christmas decorations. They were all white and silver, so it worked out well.

—Terry, mother of the bride

Pretty baskets filled with a selection of great breads were placed all around the house.

—Lara, mother of the bride

We framed childhood photos of the happy couple and displayed them on each table.

—Christine, mother of the bride

We used the favors as the decor: silver frames with Elizabeth Barrett Browning and John Browning quotes.

—Jillian, mother of the bride

One word of advice: Skip the gaudy banner, balloons, and streamers.

—Maria, mother of the groom

Invitations

You might choose to have engagement party invitations professionally printed, or you can do them up in style on your home computer. Many of the most common computer programs have invitations templates and graphics to use, so this is a fine way to save money on a necessity.

A word of caution, though: Don't put confetti, sparkles, cutouts, or any other little items inside the invitation. Many people get annoyed at having to pick them up from the floor when they open the invitation. No dust buster in the world can vacuum up all of the sparkles.

Another note of etiquette: Some people worry that their guests might consider an invitation to an engagement party a shameless request for additional gifts. While gift-giving at events like these is purely voluntary, you may wish to take the onus off the intended meaning by stating on the invitation that "no presents are necessary."

If some people do bring gifts, however, set them aside in a separate room and have the bride and groom open them privately.

Favors

The favors should reflect the formality of this event, and you should take care not to overspend on this not-too-important piece of the wedding budget. Many mothers of brides opt to make the favors, but some are able to find good bargains and high quality at craft stores and party supply houses.

Here are some ideas to get you started.

Chocolates	Miniature bottles of wine	Framed photos
Flower bulbs	Potpourri pots	Incenses
Wall hangings	Datebooks	Gourmet food baskets
Flowers	Magnets	Gift certificates

Forevergreen's Favor Ideas

Michelle Weintraub, owner of Forevergreen in Hoboken, New Jersey, recommends natural, aromatherapy-inspired, luxury products for all engagement party favors, suggested shower favors, wedding favors, and hotel room gift baskets for out-of-town guests, such as:

Aromatherapy soaps
Aromatherapy candles
Body washes
Bubble baths
Body scents

These items come in wonderful fragrances and are a true luxury. Your guests will love them. Review Forevergreen's product line at www.forevergreensoaps.com or www.soaphut.com

Entertainment

No need to hire a band or DJ for this event. Just leave a few CDs running in your CD player. Have the bride and groom supply you with a selection of their favorite music—they might agree to make a mix for you. For an inspired tribute, you and your husband can make a music mix of your own, incorporating songs that remind you of your little girl. Some suggestions: "Butterfly Kisses," "Wind Beneath My Wings," or any other appropriate title.

Toasts and Tributes

While the tears flow over the touching tunes you're dedicating to your daughter and her new husband, this is a good time to make a toast to the happy couple. This can be a hot spot between your husband and you, and between yourselves and the groom's parents, so make plans in advance either to share the spotlight or to make individual toasts throughout the night. One of the best engagement party toasts I've heard of was a running tribute that extended throughout the evening. At certain points during the event, the music was shut down for the parents of the bride to read their tribute from cards. They started with their thoughts on the day their daughter was born, waited a while (building intrigue among the guests!), went on to talk about her as a little girl, waited, talked about her high school and college years, waited, shared their take on their first impressions of her fiancé on the night of the first date, waited, then spoke of the couple's strengths and destiny for a long, happy, married life.

Your toast may not be so dramatic, but you can incorporate some of the following topics in your little speech.

- How proud you are of your daughter
- How much you like your son-in-law (don't lie, though!)
- How they have what it takes to make the marriage work
- What you hope they've learned from you
- Lessons they'll need to learn
- The joy of partnership
- Your offer of love and support in all their days
- Your best wishes

You may include song lyrics, poetry, famous quotes, even quotes from other members of the family. The idea is to personalize the moment, not to sound like a Hallmark card. Speak from your heart, don't worry if you cry, and give the happy couple a big hug and kiss afterward.

Gifts for the Couple

You and your husband will undoubtedly want to give the bride and groom an engagement gift. While many parents of brides and grooms simply hand over a sack of cash for use during the wedding, you may choose a more personal expression of your love.

Very often, the bride and groom badly need a certain item for their home. It may be a television or an entertainment center. Depending on your budget, you can surprise them with a gift certificate for their choice of that household item.

You can also give them a gift certificate to use with their bridal registry, with a note stipulating that it's to be used only after all of the showers are done. This way, the bride and groom won't snap up a large number of the affordable items that guests would be likely to buy for them. If they wait, they can get whatever hasn't been given to them, rounding out their household.

Or you can, possibly with the parents of the groom, present them with a promise to pay for their honeymoon in its entirety. At this early stage of the planning, it will greatly relieve and thrill the bride and groom to know that they will be off to sunny Jamaica after the wedding!

One touching gift I heard about: The mother of the bride gave her own mother's engagement ring to the bride for her to wear during the wedding planning process. It was an emerald ring, cut into a heart shape. You, too, might choose to gift your daughter with a touching family heirloom at this time.

Use the worksheets on pages 116–117 to organize your engagement party planning process.

Engagement Party Guest List

_____
_____
_____
_____
_____
_____
_____
_____
_____
_____
_____
_____
_____
_____
_____
_____
_____
_____
_____
_____

Engagement Party Plans

Date _____   Time _____

Place _____   Number of guests _____

Menu or caterer _____

_____

_____

Cake or dessert _____

Beverages _____

Additional shopping list _____

Decorations _____

Favors _____

Who's taking pictures/video _____

What to wear _____

Flowers/corsages _____

Invitations _____

Toast ideas _____

Gift for the couple _____

Engagement Party Gift List for Thank-Yous

Use this space to record any gift received by the bride during or before the engagement party. Here, she will have an accurate record of who gave what, so that the problem of a lost card doesn't lead to a major social gaffe. Have someone record the gifts as the bride unwraps them.

Gift	Guest	Thanked?

Special Ideas for the Engagement Party

❧

Make sure that if it's a semiformal event, you get plenty of waiters and bartenders to work through the evening. You don't want to be stuck collecting empty plates and filling glasses all night.

—Joanne, mother of the bride

❧

Who says the men always get to make the big toasts? I say, let the mother of the bride propose a toast as well!

—Lara, mother of the bride

❧

Get it all on videotape as well as in snapshots. It will be fun, at the end of the whole wedding and after the honeymoon, to be able to sit down and watch yourselves throughout the whole process. Plus, you'll get to see how calm and beautiful you looked that night!

—Patricia, mother of the bride

❧

Spend some time with the bride and groom alone after the party is over—and not just cleaning up. Talk about how nice the night was.

—Annalise, mother of the bride

❧

Even if there's no dance floor, encourage spontaneous slow-dancing to the music that is playing. The guests will join in, and everyone will want to get pictures of you dancing with your soon-to-be son-in-law.

—Kelly, mother of the bride

Mingle! Laugh! Have fun! Enjoy yourself!

—Jessica, mother of the bride

8

What to Wear

BECAUSE EVERYONE HAS his or her own wardrobe for the wedding, we'll break this down into the various areas, advising you of your part in selection and delivery. As the bride's helper, you may be called upon to help with the selections, ordering, running around, confirmations, and people-handling. So, you'll need to know the ins and outs of each wedding wardrobe category.

The Bride

She has her own books and articles describing the perfect gown for her, so you'll have little to do in terms of the actual selection. This doesn't mean your daughter doesn't want your opinion, and, of course, you may be called upon to break a tie between two or three perfect gowns. Or you may be needed to help search for a particular style and size in a store near you. Your role in this process will be decided primarily by the bride, as her gown is usually the biggest and most important part of this wedding to her. It's a reflection of her style, her tastes—how she's looked in her dreams and now it's become a reality.

Nothing is more special or enjoyable between a mother and daughter than that big shopping trip to the bridal boutiques, when your little girl twirls around in front of a three-way mirror in countless breathtaking gowns and headpieces.

That's when it all seemed so real, seeing my little girl trying on her gown. When she found the perfect one I just knew it, and the tears started to flow.

—Maria, mother of the bride

My mom initially didn't like my gown. I'd seen it in a magazine, found it in one store, and it was the only one I tried on. I just knew it was the gown for me, but she kept fighting me, telling me to try some more on. I didn't because I knew what was right for me. We got into a little fight, but eventually my mom agreed that the gown was perfect.

—Ashley, bride

Most brides and mothers of brides will advise you not to miss the big trying-on days. It is a bonding experience, something your daughter has been looking forward to, perhaps for years. While she's standing in front of the mirror in the gown she loves, she'll be searching for the look of happiness in your eyes. Where mothers and daughters clash, however, is usually when the mother attempts to assert some control or judgment over the bride's choices. The bride may look for your approval, but she's doing this because she's nervous about the choice, not because she wants you to choose for her. This is a very important task for her. Standing up there in that wedding gown can be as frightening as it is exciting. For the first time, she's seeing herself as "the bride," and that can be overwhelming. So if your daughter truly loves

a gown you don't particularly care for, think about your reasons for not liking it. Judge whether it's because you don't like the gown for your tastes. Remember, your daughter has a style of her own, and she wants to make her wedding gown meaningful to reflect who she is.

If your daughter has asked to wear your gown or another family heirloom dress, enjoy the moment. But never attempt to push that choice on her. It is her day, her choice. You are not there to make the decision more difficult.

❧

I would never dream of asking my daughter to wear my gown, even though that's what I really, really would have wanted, if it had been up to me. When she asked, I nearly fainted from happiness! It didn't matter that the dress didn't fit. We found an excellent seamstress and MADE it work.

—Jane, mother of the bride

❧

Things to Remember When Choosing a Wedding Gown

- The season. Is it the right dress for a summer wedding? Is it too summery for a winter wedding?
- The weather. Will the dress be too heavy for a warm day? Too light for a cold day?
- Appropriate cut of the dress. Is it too revealing, too tight, too low-cut?

- Comfort. Is the bride itchy? Can she sit, move, dance, bend over? If the bride is short, make sure there's no easy view down the front of her gown for taller guests.
- Simpler is most often better. Who wants to look like a chandelier?
- The right style for the bride's body shape—some necklines or skirt shapes hide or accentuate figure flaws
- A good seamstress can add accents and details, and any number of alterations can make the cut perfect.
- Go for gown try-ons at the beginning of the day, after a light breakfast or lunch, so that the bride has enough energy to devote to the job.

For Your Information

Wearing white is no longer the rule for first-time brides. Henry Weinreich of Michelle Roth Studio in Manhattan says that ivories, beiges, and even pale rose colors are in fashion now, and all meaning attached to the bride's virginal status has been removed by the dictates of fashion. So, if your daughter wants to wear off-white, don't worry about what Grandma will think. Allow your daughter to make this choice as it pleases her.

The Bridal Party

Again, the bride and bridesmaids will have their own pick of that wonderful selection of bridesmaids' gowns. Your part may come in when it's time to coordinate the ordering and delivery.

If the women are all in different locations, different states, maybe even different countries, remind the bride that all of the maids' dresses should be ordered from the same location to ensure that the dye lots will be the same. Otherwise, you'll have varying degrees of color, making some look faded, others too vibrant. A simple solution: Have the bridesmaids get their exact measurements taken by a professional seamstress, then send their size cards to you or to the bride, who will place one big order with the store. Do not just let the girl guess her size. It's a mistake to accept "I'm a size 7, so order me a 7." Bridesmaids' gowns are notorious for running as many as ten sizes small, especially if you've ordered a junior-style dress. Remind the bride of this if she's tempted to take the quick route and just order by everyday dress size. You've just avoided a major catastrophe.

❧

My mission is to make sure this doesn't happen to anyone else. One of my bridesmaids asked all the other girls their sizes, and she ordered my sister's dress six sizes too small. Even worse, my sister was upset that she'd gained some weight after a miscarriage, So when the dress didn't even close around her, and there was no time left to order a different dress, my poor sister had to wear a similar but different dress than everyone else's. It was horrible for her.

—Patricia, bride

❧

The Men

From the groom to the ushers to the fathers of the bride and groom, all of the men have to be dressed in a uniform style, if not in identical tuxes. The bride and groom get to pick the color and style they prefer for their wedding party look.

The work comes in when it's time to get the men's sizes. Again, have them all go out and get their measurements taken professionally, recorded on size cards, and sent to you. Place their orders all at once, and arrange for someone else to pick them up and drop them off afterward. (This might be a good job for the father of the bride—he can go with all of the men to their fittings as well.) Don't forget shoe sizes if renting uniform black dress shoes. Let the men try on the shoes beforehand as well, and make sure they have black socks!

Be sure the groomsmen have a definite plan for dropping off the tuxes the next morning. Check for all accessories, and be sure they don't forget the shoes. No one will be in the mood for hunting down, chasing, and having to drive all the way back to the hotel to pick up a forgotten bow tie.

The Flower Girl and Ring Bearer

The bride may opt to leave it all up to the kids' parents to dress them in an appropriate style and color. Perhaps the kids can get a second use out of a Communion outfit or a dress for another wedding or formal event. No one will tell.

The little ones may wear a corresponding style to that of the bridal party wardrobe, so make sure the flower girl is brought to the salon for the choosing and alteration of her dress. But unless her mother is in the bridal party herself, let the poor, harried woman know that it's okay for her to leave early with the little girl. There's no need to force the child to hang around if it's not necessary.

Your Dress

Of course, you want to look lovely on the day of the wedding, but you also have to go along with the rules of formality of the day. If the bride is in an informal, simple dress, you should by no means arrive in a beaded, spangled dress worthy of the Oscars. You can look beautiful without outshining the bride.

You, too, will be bound by the fashion mores of formal versus informal. Follow these dress rules, so that you can choose a dress that's right for the style of event.

- Informal: Street dress or casual suit
- Semiformal: Casual suit, tea-length dress
- Formal: Cocktail-length dress or full-length gown
- Ultraformal: Full-length gown

Once you know what style of dress is necessary, and what color you and the mother of the groom will be wearing, allow yourself plenty of time to try on dresses. Visit several different stores until you find the perfect dress for you. Your daughter may want you to wear a certain color—or *not* to wear a certain color—so you must go by her wishes. You may have to coordinate dress colors with the mother of the groom, which again may be the bride's wish.

Search for your dress the way the bride searches for hers, just not at the same time she's searching for hers. Her quest for the perfect gown is her special moment. She will look to you for your involvement in her choice, and she won't want to wait while you're running through the racks, absorbed in your own search.

Look through magazines for the perfect styles; hunt through the racks at regular department stores' formal sections; try on and try on until you find a dress that flatters you and makes you feel wonderful. Believe me, having on a great new outfit and knowing you look good will take away some of the wedding day jitters.

Allow time for fittings, but do them on your own time, and invite your daughter to your final fitting. Ask her to help you pick out accessories. Include her in your choices as she's included you in hers. This will make her feel needed, and it will remind her at this important time that she is in charge here.

❧

The biggest fight my mom and I had was when she refused to wear the color gown I asked her to wear. It had come at a time when all my other requests were getting shot down, too, so I just lost it. It wouldn't have killed her just to wear the color dress I asked for. Worse yet, my husband's mother joined forces with Mom and wouldn't wear that color either. I was so angry, and to this day she justifies her position. She wound up getting a pretty dress, but it wasn't worth hurting me so much.

—Angela, bride

❧

Colors to Stay Away From

- White. Only the bride should be in white. This is not a time for you to look like twins.
- Black. It may be a "black and white wedding," but black is too clichéd, as suggesting the disapproving mother-in-law.
- Red. It just screams "pool hall."
- Neon brights. Obviously.

You know by now which colors suit your skin shade, so go with something that you know will work for you. It is not necessary for you to match the bridal party's color. Indeed, you should be in a complementary color so that you stand out in the pictures.

Look back at the list of things to remember when choosing the bride's dress, and see if they apply to your choice of dress. Is it appropriate for the season and the weather? Is it comfortable? Can you move in it? Is it too revealing?

This last question is a big sticking point for brides. You may not be the type of mom to flaunt your assets, but many a bride has complained that her mother "showed her up" at the wedding. Perhaps the mother's gown was too revealing, or it was just far more ornate and eye-catching than the bride's simple sheath.

Here is a wedding nightmare that should be avoided at all costs. One bride reported that her mother pressured her to buy a less expensive gown, claiming that the budget was just pulled too tight for an expensive dress. At the end of the wedding planning process, it turned out that there was a good-sized chunk of cash left over. Stealthily, the mother of the bride spent that money on a designer dress that cost more than the bride's gown. Five times more. The bride found out and was crushed. Sounds impossible to you? The mother who did this said she wasn't trying to be selfish. She was just caught up in the moment. After all those months of hard work, she just wanted to splurge a little. The bride's response: *"Whatever, Mom."*

Always get your daughter's approval of what you're going to wear. Don't tell her it's a surprise. Brides don't want to be surprised. Check with her, and make sure she likes it.

Wedding Dress Fittings Schedule

Date _____

Time _____

Work to Be Done _____

Cost _____

Date _____

Time _____

Work to Be Done _____

Cost _____

Date _____

Time _____

Work to Be Done _____

Cost _____

Date _____

Time _____

Work to Be Done _____

Cost _____

Bridal Clothes Pickup/Drop-Off Worksheet

Items _____

Pick up _____

Drop-off _____

By Whom _____

Items _____

Pick up _____

Drop-off _____

By Whom _____

Items _____

Pick up _____

Drop-off _____

By Whom _____

Items _____

Pick up _____

Drop-off _____

By Whom _____

9

Invitations, Responses, and Programs

YOU MAY BE ASKED for your input regarding the selection of the wedding invitations, especially since they likely will be worded to come from you and your husband. The bride and groom will be faced with hundreds, if not thousands, of choices, and they'll want your opinion to narrow it down. Of course, personal preference is the rule here, but you may want to keep these hints in mind:

1. Less is more. Go for a simple, elegant style. Leave the pastel love birds for the wrapping paper.
2. Consider the cost. What will 300 of these things run you?
3. Know exactly how many you'll need before you order. Countless brides have a box of fifty unused invitations among their keepsakes.
4. Order several extra invitations. Make allowances for spelling mistakes and coffee drips.
5. Check and double-check your wording. Printed mistakes cannot be erased.

131

6. Copy the wording style from an example in the invitation book or consult an etiquette book for the correct wording for your personal life situation (see examples in this chapter). Etiquette books will instruct you how to address envelopes, what abbreviations to spell out, and so on.

7. Keep all copies of your original contract and the receipt from your order. Get the name of the person who took your order, and keep careful track of your payments.

Invitation Wording

On the left-hand side of page 133 is an example of the wording of a standard wedding invitation. That is, the bride's married parents are the hosts of the event. If the couple is hosting the wedding, the wording of the invitation should read as the one on the right.

For a formal wedding, etiquette will dictate wording and spelling. For a less formal affair, feel free to use less-constrained, though appropriate, wording, such as "Anne Smith and Steven Johnson invite you to attend the celebration of their marriage," and so on. The bride and groom will certainly have their own wishes regarding the style and wording of the invitations, but if you are listed on the invitation as hostess, you do have some veto power. You may have valid concerns about the invitation seeming too informal for the style of wedding you have planned, so it is in the best interest of all to bring this to the bride and groom's attention—diplomatically, of course.

Invitation Tips

1. People over eighteen years of age get their own invitation, according to tradition.

2. Allow plenty of RSVP time, at least eight weeks.

Mr. and Mrs. John Smith

request the honour of your presence

at the marriage of their daughter

Anne Elizabeth Smith

and

Steven Andrew Johnson

son of

Mr. and Mrs. Andrew Johnson

Thursday, the twelfth of February,

at six o'clock in the evening

Sts. Peter and Paul Church

New York, New York

Ms. Anne Elizabeth Smith

and

Mr. Steven Andrew Johnson

request the honour of your presence

at their marriage

Thursday, the twelfth of February,

at six o'clock in the evening

Sts. Peter and Paul Church

New York, New York

3. Be sure the stamps have been affixed to the response cards. Forgetting this step could result in delayed responses.
4. Make sure all maps, menu choice cards, reception cards, and extras are included in the envelopes before sealing.
5. If hiring a calligrapher, just give her the envelopes to work on, not all the elements of the invitations package.

6. Be sure you know your guests' true titles. That is, if someone is a doctor, address his envelope to Dr. Smith. Don't forget about lawyers (Esquire), military personnel (Captain—make sure they haven't recently been promoted!), ministers, rabbis, judges, and so forth.

7. Make sure there is adequate postage on each invitation package. Take one to the post office to weigh it before stamping all of the others.

8. Use post office "Love" stamps, rather than standard stamps. Some post offices also have stamps that correspond to a wedding's theme, such as angels, ballet, holidays, and so on.

Tips to Organize Wedding Responses

Keep a yes–no checkoff column on your master list, or you could do as you've seen in movies: Have a "yes" shoebox and a "no" shoebox. Many brides record the yesses and nos on the top lid of the shoebox as they toss the response cards in. Check, double-check, and triple-check your head count so that you'll be accurate when ordering food, cake, beverages, favors, and so forth.

If, at the RSVP date, some guests have not responded, it is perfectly proper to give the guests a call to check for their answers. Just do so in a friendly manner, not an accusatory tone. The guests should know by now if they will be attending, and they'll be sure to understand your "need to know" status. Don't worry about offending people. If you are diplomatic, and if they've ever planned a wedding, they will understand.

What if someone who didn't respond says he never got a wedding invitation? It has happened, as reliable as the postal system usually is. Apologize profusely, and send out another invitation right away. Let him know that he has always been on the wedding list, and that this was simply one of those unavoidable problems. Unfortunately, you may get some attitude if this comes up. People can be, by nature, very cynical, and this supposed snub is just a reason for them to enjoy being miserable. So do your part to remedy the situation, and let it go. Don't grovel. Don't crawl to make it up. Just send out a new invite, and move on. You have much bigger things to think about.

Wedding Programs

A nice touch at the ceremony is to hand out wedding programs. Much like a theater program, a wedding program lists the elements of the ceremony and can include some other nice touches.

1. The participants: bride, groom, bridal party, officiant, performers, and parents of the bride and groom
2. The order of events: From the Processional to the Recessional, the main points in the ceremony are listed so that the individual readings and rituals are explained to the guests.
3. Any rules the wedding location may have, such as no taking pictures, no throwing birdseed, and so forth
4. A special poem the bride and groom have chosen to share
5. A special note from the bride and groom
6. The bride and groom's address after the wedding

If ordering programs, compare widely. Many professionally printed programs are expensive, and they come out just as nicely if you make them yourself with a computer, printer, a discount printer for multiple copies, and perhaps a store-bought program cover found at a religious bookstore or bridal shop.

❧

We made our programs with our computer, and it was so much fun to design it ourselves and put them all together. It turned out to be a great creative outlet for us, one of the only truly personalized parts of our day.
—Nina, bride

❧

At the ceremony, have a special cousin or friend hand out the programs to each guest, or to each family—specify ahead of time!—and preside over the guest book. Perhaps the guest book can be a touching little gift to the bride from you, as a way to tell her you've enjoying working with her on this wedding, and you hope she'll remember it forever.

10

The Bridal Registry

THE BRIDE AND GROOM WILL no doubt wish to register for all the things they'll need to set up their new home. Nowadays, there are more places to register than just the silver and china sections of major department stores. Your daughter may already be set up in life, complete with a fully stocked home of her own. She may not need bath towels and a set of everyday plates. So, search around for other places they may wish to register.

There are sporting goods shops, if your daughter and her husband love the active life. Music and video stores supply entertainment needs. Hardware stores even have registries now. You can find a complete list of wedding registries, descriptions, and contact information in *The Bridal Registry Book,* by Leah Ingram (Contemporary Books). Check out this title for additional registry ideas to suggest to the bride and groom.

As for their choices of everyday items, here you can be of some assistance. Having kept a home of your own for more than twenty years, you undoubtedly know the ins and outs of housewares. You may be able to give them valuable advice on what to register for and what not to. You know your favorite items and brand names, so you can make recommendations that will help them avoid the lemons in the marketplace.

But beware. While you may have the best of intentions, this may be one area that the bride and groom will simply not want to be caught in the middle of a lot of friendly "helpers." They may have compromised on every decision until now and will just not want to have you telling them what color of towels to buy. Indeed, they are perfectly justified in not wanting any buttinskys interfering in what is supposed to be a pleasant outing.

You can help, however, by approaching the bride at the right time, when she is relaxed, and saying nicely, "I know you're planning to register soon, and if you'd like any recommendations as far as brands and the like, I'm here to help." Throw in this one for good measure: "I know your father and I made a lot of mistakes with our registry, and we don't want you to walk that same road." No child wants to walk the same road as her parents, even if it's paved with gold. If you calmly suggest that you have some insight for her when she's ready, she'll be more likely to come to you for a friendly discussion. Let her know that you can save her money and help her get better quality, without it resembling the style of decor you have. That'll do it.

Here are some topics you might address with her before she and her fiancé set out to register.

The Real Kitchen Needs

Search your own experiences. A fondue pot may have sounded like a good idea when you registered for your wedding, but you've only used it once and considered it too much trouble. You know the best kinds of cookware, the difference between Calphalon and regular stainless steel. You know what prices are worth the quality of product. Talk with your daughter and her fiancé about the practicality of a rice cooker, when those 1-minute bags of Uncle Ben's are easier on frantic schedules. You also know the complete list of necessary kitchen gadgets. Beyond spatulas and measuring cups, you might have experience in knowing that a shrimp deveiner is the most ridiculous invention ever. A lemon zester? Champagne bottle stopper? Apple peeler? Your knowledge can save them from wasting their registry on unimportant items, making sure that they receive shower and wedding gifts they will need and use. This is advice your daughter can only get from you, the kind of thing she doesn't have the life knowledge to realize right now.

Linens

You've bought sheets and blankets for years. You know the difference between percale and Egyptian cotton. You know which sheet brands hold up after repeated washings. You know which blankets are the best, and which are not. You also know how many sets of sheets are really needed. You know to remind them to get summer sheets *and* winter flannels, something they may not be thinking about in the warm month of May. Teach them the difference between quality towels and the cheap kinds that will pill. Tell them about the real need for hand towels. Talk to them about shower curtain liners and machine-washable shower curtains.

China and Crystal

There's not much you can say here. It is up to the bride and groom to choose a style that suits their tastes. If they pick the black and white cubism set, that is their decision. It is not your place to whine, "But what about business dinners?" You can, however, use your own experience in knowing that some of the expensive extras, such as multiple serving platters, are just too much and not practical. It is not necessary to get salt and pepper shakers that match the set. A standard set of glass salt and pepper shakers (for $5 at a discount store) will do.

Flatware

You can remind them to get the shrimp forks, the salad forks, the serving spoons, anything they'll need. For everyday flatware, encourage them to buy brands you know and love. Advise them to avoid the kind of flatware that has two parts, that is, the stainless steel of the fork and knife are connected by a rivet to the handle. After repeated washing, the rivet rusts and the forks and knives fall apart.

Home Decor

If they register for home decor, such as lamps, figurines, and so forth, tell them to get the store UPC code of the item, so that guests do not buy any old lamp or statue. Advise them to note their room themes, such as ducks or lighthouses, on the registry, so that guests pick suitable items.

Appliances

Tell them your favorite brands, the ones you've researched through *Consumer Reports* or other guides. After years of trial and error, you know which brands outlast the others, which have better warranties, and which are worth the money. Tell them which appliances are necessary. Tell them that a rug shampooer can be rented at the local Costco. Explain that they need vacuum cleaner bags as well as the vacuum.

Registry Tips

- Remind them to state their color choices on the registry, so that all of their linens match.
- Remind them to take stock of what they already own, and not to double-register.
- Remind them to include in the registry where to send the gifts. If the bride will be moving, say, after college graduation, have the gifts sent to the groom's home or to yours. Faraway guests will appreciate having the store ship the gifts directly to you.
- Don't treat them like children. They may have run their own place for a while, even if it hasn't been to your standards. Although they are just starting out, they know what most items are used for. Yes, you want to be helpful, but in some instances you can cross the line and be insulting. Remember, they will be high-strung, and any implied threat to their capabilities is likely to earn you a good snapping or two. Even if they don't know the difference

between a bread board and a cutting board, they are still two adults and should be spoken to as such.

◆ Remember that just as this is not your wedding to plan, this is not your home to furnish. Don't get swept up in the details. Don't demand to see the registry when they get it home, and don't criticize choices. A big mistake made by parents is saying, "We have those here. You could have taken them. Why'd you waste your time registering for that?" Don't question the kids' choices. Just decide what you're going to get them.

The place where they register will further assist the bride and groom through the process of choosing what to include in their computer file. Most places are consumer-friendly and act like Rodeo Drive salons, assigning personal shoppers and researchers who will run to find the perfect matching items. It is indeed a fun outing for the bride and groom, as they are treated like royalty by a staff who is there to serve them. You've seen the countless happy brides- and grooms-to-be walking through these stores with clipboards and pencils, or handheld scanners, scribbling down their choices, dreaming of their ideal future home. Your daughter and new son-in-law will enjoy this day trip. Why not treat them to lunch afterward?

Announcing the Registry

How do you let people know where the bride is registered? It used to be considered very tacky, as if it were a plea for presents. No more. Now, guests want to know where she's registered, so they'll be sure to get her what she really needs. No one wants to give the bride something she hates and ultimately has to return. So have the bridesmaids print "Registered at Macy's" on the shower invitation. It's simple, it's not a plea, and guests will be glad to have that information, should they choose to use it.

An additional benefit to the bridal registry list: What's left on the list remains in the file for up to a year after the wedding (some places keep it longer, if asked). Get a printout so that your next gifts to the newlyweds—say, for birthdays or holidays—can be even more items that they wished for.

11

No Men Allowed

SOME EVENTS ARE JUST GIRLS ONLY: showers, bachelorette parties, the bridal luncheon. This is downtime for the women, when they can converse about men and relationships, keeping a home, or even raising children, without the judgmental raising of eyebrows by the various men in their lives. By their very nature, these are bonding rituals that reach back to ancient times, when the women of the community would take time to lead the bride through rituals, pamper her, and gift her with items for her dowry. Showers and bachelorette parties also have their origins in past eras, and indeed many of the games and old wives' tales that remain hearken back to the days when women blessed a marriage through various traditions.

The Bridal Shower

The most enduring women's ritual is the bridal shower. According to tradition, the mother of the bride doesn't give her daughter a bridal shower. Etiquette mavens say that's tacky, a true plea for gifts. So you're off the hook here. You may be asked for your opinion and assistance by the bridesmaids

or any of the bride's friends or relatives, but it is not your place to take the reins here. Don't be offended, though. Think of this as you should: It's just one thing you don't have to worry about. The bridesmaids will do a fine job of organizing it. All you have to do is show up, unless you've been asked for your input.

If you've been asked to help out, consider several ideas for shower themes, locations, and favors. If the theme is rainbows, consider serving rainbow trout, rainbow sherbet, and multicolored jello shapes. Have a rainbow painted in frosting on the cake, and give out prisms as favors to the guests. Hung in the window, they catch the sunlight and toss rainbows onto the floor. Have "Somewhere Over the Rainbow" be on the CD player when the bride walks in.

If butterflies are the theme, serve sweet fruits that butterflies like, have the butter pats molded into the appropriate shapes for spreading on breads, decorate a butterfly on the sheet cake. Some creative bridal parties hold the shower of this theme in a butterfly garden, with hundreds of butterflies, in their natural habitat, fluttering about. Give out butterfly hairpins and clips, butterfly T-shirts, even a copy of Mariah Carey's CD *Butterfly.*

Obviously, you can turn any theme into an opportunity to flex your creative muscles. Just be sure to give the bridal party the same treatment you gave the bride; Do not steamroll everyone's plans either. If you have been asked for ideas, the best bet is to write down your ideas and give them to the maid of honor or hostess of the party. Do not call every ten minutes with additional ideas, or you will become a victim of the gossip line. Just be helpful, answer questions, tell them you're there for them if you're needed, and then step back and let them run the show.

Perhaps you can offer to make the favors as your contribution to the party. Being short on cash and time, the bridesmaids may go for that. Perhaps you'll agree to be part of the surprise plan, asking your daughter out to lunch when she least expects a shower and delivering her into it. Or, you can simply help set up on the day of the party, as everyone scrambles to cover the last details.

Be sure to bring your camera or a video camera to capture these moments. The bride will love seeing this event on film, particularly her moment of surprise, as she may not remember it all too well right then.

My daughter's bridesmaids needed help with the shower, since they were all in college and couldn't do the legwork or the financing. My husband and I were glad to help, and we avoided any problems by putting only the bridesmaids' names on the invitation as hostesses. It avoided criticism and helped out the girls who were so upset that they couldn't do it all—and I got to plan my own little party! I was glad they asked me to help!

—Donna, mother of the bride

❧

By this time, I was so grateful not *to have to do something that I was glad to let the bridesmaids take over and do the whole thing!*

—Cathy, mother of the bride

❧

Your gift to the bride may be something special, like the honeymoon-night peignoir. Some mothers of the bride go all out shopping for shower gifts. That's completely up to you—you may need a good shopping trip by now.

The most important thing to remember is that you are not the hostess of this event. The maid of honor and the bridesmaids are hosting. They get the floor at the beginning of the event. They make the speeches. They run the games. They say when it's okay to hit the buffet line. It may feel unnatural to you to have a bunch of twenty-somethings in control of an event at which you feel you should have a place of honor. You do have a place of honor. It is in being the mother of the bride.

So do not sit there in resentment at being left out of the plans. Just enjoy the fact that your daughter has such wonderful friends to do this for her. Look at the smile on your daughter's face as she opens her gifts. Mingle with other guests, but don't gab about your huge responsibilities in planning the wedding. Since it is so close to the date of the wedding, your patience may be worn thin as well, but you can do yourself and your daughter no greater service than to be a smiling, supportive mom right now. Even if the bridesmaids tell some off-color stories about your daughter, keep your sense of humor, shake your head, and allow the girls to have fun.

Speaking of keeping your sense of humor and allowing the girls to have some fun, let's talk about the bachelorette party.

The Bachelorette Party

This all-girl fling is something you might not choose to take part in. Depending on the personalities of your daughter and her friends, the evening can be filled with alcohol, dancing, and flirtation. They may even hire a male stripper or go to a male strip show. While some more progressive moms do attend these events, you'll need to assess your comfort level as well as your daughter's. She may say it's fine for you to go, but your presence may make her feel she has to be more reserved.

Some bachelorette's parties are getting racier. It's not uncommon for the bride to wear a T-shirt onto which candies have been attached. Male bar patrons are encouraged to bite a candy off the shirt for a dollar. More strategically placed candies are worth five dollars. Brides-to-be are often called upon to dance on the bar, lick tequila off the bartender's neck, or do a shot from between a bartender's legs. In other words, it ain't pretty.

Before you roll your eyes to think of your daughter acting this way, know that it's her last hurrah, and she's unlikely to do anything that will raise the dead, so to speak. So let her have her one night of unbridled fun, know that you brought her up well, and think about whether or not you want to be around for any of it.

One excellent solution is for you and the mother of the groom to join the girls for dinner and a few drinks at the beginning of the evening. Have a blast with the girls, then send them off to their own celebration. You've been a part of the night, and now it's time to bow out gracefully.

While you are not to be Policewoman Mom, you should make sure that a safe driver has been assigned for the night. Many bridal parties book a limo or a party bus to take them club-hopping. Be sure there's a designated driver (who won't be drinking), or that the girls have booked a hotel room for their safe lodging.

If you're worried about your daughter—or your son-in-law—dancing with a greased-up stripper, take heart. A growing trend today is to have a combined bachelor/bachelorette party, where everyone goes out to dance, celebrate, and have a good time together. The strippers will not be a part of it, the candy shirt is likely to stay in the drawer, and no one has to worry what the other half of the couple is up to.

❧

I was so glad to hear that my son-in-law didn't want a big bachelor party. I figured, if he's in love with my daughter, he wouldn't want a last fling. He made serious points with me by wanting a group party.
—Helen, mother of the bride

❧

Like my daughter, I wasn't worried about her fiancé going out with the guys. He's a good man. He's loved my daughter for years. He wouldn't behave badly. He'd just better not show up drunk at the wedding.
—Anita, mother of the bride

❧

That big night out was just what we all needed.
—Stephanie, bride

❧

You probably won't have much planning power here, but it would be wise of you to voice your opinion that the bachelor/bachelorette's parties be held a week, or at least a few days, before the wedding. Too many night-before-the-wedding parties get wild, and the bride and groom are either hungover, sick, or still drunk on the wedding day. The kids are well aware of this, and they may be receptive to having it the day before the rehearsal or the weekend before the wedding, if they haven't planned to already.

Another option that is becoming more popular, especially among older brides and grooms who have been out of college for a while, is to skip the drinking and partying and do something fun together as a group. Many brides report that they went to a spa for a weekend with their bridal parties, enjoying all of the luxury pampering available. Both the men and the women also go to various sporting events, such as baseball or football games. They may choose to get Broadway play tickets, take a weekend trip to the shore, go camping, go on a dinner cruise, or go skiing.

The Bridal Luncheon

On the morning of the wedding, the women will gather at the bride's home to get ready and to help the bride get ready. They may all go to the salon to have their hair and nails done, but when they return, it is a very good idea to have a bridal luncheon waiting for them.

Everyone will be nervous and excited on the morning of the wedding, so make sure that people have plenty to eat. Being well nourished will help the bride and her attendants—and yourself—have energy for the day, and it will keep them from getting weak or passing out during the ceremony. Make sure everyone drinks plenty of water and juice, and limit the coffee for those with already-frazzled nerves.

You might serve a selection of somewhat bland foods, such as lots of breads, bagels, and eggs, things that are not too spicy or heavy. And by all means, have everyone eat *before* they get dressed!

Since the men have to eat, too, you should arrange with the caterer, or with a helpful friend, to have some food sent over to where the men are getting ready for the wedding. No need to leave them out.

This is quite often a fun breakfast. People are chatty and look forward to the day. There may be a surreal feeling to the morning; everyone knows that after these long months of planning, the moment is finally here. Just enjoy this last sit-down together with the bride and the bridal party, and enjoy everyone's happiness.

12

Transportation and Lodging for All

CONSIDER YOURSELF THE STAGE MANAGER of the wedding production. It is your job to make sure all of the "players" are in the right place at the right time. Thus, it falls upon you to arrange for all of the necessary transportation and lodging for your guests. The bride has way too many things to take care of at this point, and you already have direction skills from your days as a soccer mom or the driver of Mom's taxi service. While you may not do the actual driving, it's your job to take pencil in hand and arrange for all of the correct pickups, drop-offs, and lodging for your guests and the bridal party. These people have to stay somewhere, and if you don't want them in your house, eating your food, you'll have to get them accommodations that suit their needs.

Is it still the bride's family's responsibility to pay for the travel and lodging for all the out-of-town guests? That's everyone on our list, practically! Etiquette mavens may say yes to this, but are they going to foot the bill for all the airline tickets? Make this a selective thing. If you have family or friends who des-

148

perately need help paying their way, and it's important to the bride and groom to have them there, by all means help out if you can. For all others, just don't mention it. Let them fend for themselves.

In this chapter, you'll organize the entire schedule, meeting every need, so no one is left stranded.

Transportation

One of the most involving and tricky issues you'll encounter when putting the wedding together is choreographing how to get everyone from place to place. It may be obvious that you'll need to get to the ceremony on time, but there are many other pickups and drop-offs you'll have to arrange as well.

The entire job may be a matter of finding out airline arrival times and gates, booking limos or town cars to go get them, asking helpful relatives or friends to do the driving, or allowing the guests to take a cab. If you have a lot of guests, and if many are from out-of-town, this scheduling can be a hair-raising experience. You may have as many as twenty pickups to handle on the day before the wedding. So be organized, get all your information together, and get ready to delegate—or make some bookings.

Here, then, are some ideas to think about and space to record your plans and assignments.

Pickup and Drop-off Arrangements

Bride and groom coming into town _____

Bride coming into town _____

Groom coming into town _____

Bridal party coming into town _____

_____

_____

_____

_____

Groom's family coming into town _____

_____

_____

Groom's family for the rehearsal _____

Bride and groom for the rehearsal _____

Bridal party for the rehearsal _____

Parents for the rehearsal _____

Family/friends without rides to the rehearsal _____

Rides to the rehearsal dinner _____

_____

Rides for the bachelorette's party _____

_____

Rides for the bachelor's party _____

_____

Groom's family to the wedding _____

Groom's parents to the wedding _____

Groom to the wedding _____

Groomsmen to the wedding _____

Bridesmaids to the wedding _____

Bride's parents to the wedding _____

Bride to the wedding _____

Family/friends without rides to the wedding _____

Parents to the reception _____

Groom's family to the reception _____

Bridal party to the reception _____

Family/friends without rides to the reception _____

Bride and groom after the reception _____

Parents after the reception _____

Groom's family after the reception _____

Bridal party after the reception _____

Family/friends without rides after the reception _____

Bride and groom to the airport/train station for the honeymoon _____

Bridal party returned home _____

Groom's family returned home _____

Parents returned home _____

Family/friends returned home _____

Once you know exactly what kind of transportation you will need and when you'll need it, you're ready to begin searching for rides. There's no rule saying that anyone has to have limousine service. It would be fine to have only the bride delivered to the wedding in a limo, and the bride and groom delivered to the reception in it as well, but even that's not a necessity. Many brides and grooms prefer to go in their own nice car or a friend's, an arrangement that allows for the JUST MARRIED signs and the dragging tin cans.

The hotel we chose for our guests had a shuttle bus service that actually took them to and from the airport and carted them around town to all the shopping areas during downtime. Then, we scheduled it to bring them to and from the wedding and reception. It was wonderful!

—Karon, bride

Don't be surprised if you have to do some unexpected last-minute switches and scrambling. When dealing with transportation, much like traffic, you just never know. Flights are delayed, cars get lost, people miss their trains. Make sure that everyone has your phone number, and that you have some way to get them to where they need to be. If no ride is available, you might have to tell your guests to grab a cab and then reimburse them for the fare when you see them.

Some Things to Remember About Rides

- Ask if you'll need baby seats for transporting infants and toddlers.
- Ask your inbound guests to confirm their flights ahead of time.
- Ask your guests to meet you at the baggage carousel. Most airports no longer let nonticketed guests past the security checkpoints.
- Don't be afraid to delegate: This is a great job for the best man to do. (Let him do *something* besides make a toast at the reception!)
- If the bride and groom offer to help out, let them. It may be a time of great excitement for them to meet their favorite people at the airport.
- Make sure your drivers have cell phones with them, in case you get a call from rerouted travelers.
- Keep everything in writing. You're the dispatcher, and you'll need to make sure all customers are satisfied.

My husband and I told his brothers and sisters that they could make their wedding gift to us their presence at the wedding. For all of them to come, round-trip, it would cost them in the thousands of dollars, so we didn't want them to spend a dime more. It turned out to be just the break they needed, and we had our whole family together. It was a priceless, precious gift, better than any trinket or check they might have handed us.

—Shea, bride

❧

Lodging

No one says you have to pay for them, but finding places for everyone to stay will fall into your realm of responsibility, especially if the bride and groom are bogged down with their own jobs. So start your search off with a clean comparison worksheet (see page 158), and call around town to find the best deal in a nice area of town.

❧

We found the lowest price in town, all right, but then we were horrified to learn that my mother-in-law saw cockroaches in her room and had to switch hotels on her own.

—Dede, bride

❧

Always go with a hotel that has a good reputation, perhaps a starred rating in travel books. You can't miss with reputable hotel chains. Avoid the travel lodge on the main highway. You know, the one with the flickering lights out front and the sign that says HBO IN ALL ROOMS! It may be closest to the reception hall, but your guests will not be happy with the "creature comforts" of *that* home for the weekend.

Assessing Hotels

- Always go for a visit in person.
- Make sure it's rated with AAA or some other travel bureau.
- Look for cleanliness and friendly service.
- Look at the rooms in person.
- Check out the pool and gym to be sure they're clean and in working order.
- Check out the hotel's restaurant or room-service menu. You don't want your guests to be unable to get juice or a snack when needed.
- Does the hotel offer free shuttle service?
- Are entrances to the rooms onto the street or the parking lot, or are they internal entrances? Some people worry about break-ins when entrances to the rooms are on the street.
- Is the place well lit?
- How does it smell? Some hotels with indoor pools have a chlorine smell.
- What will travel be like between the reception site and the hotel? Perilous intersections? Winding roads? Remember, your guests might not know their way around.
- Is there adequate parking?
- Is it in a safe area of town?
- Are there blow-driers in the bathrooms? Robes? Toiletries?
- Would you stay there?

❧

We found this out the hard way. Make sure the hotel is not one of those sex-oriented places. Our guests were not happy that there were quarter slots above the bed, condom dispensers in the bathroom, and the sounds of sex going on in the next room. We were amused, but they weren't.

—Lana, bride

❧

If you'll be booking a large number of rooms, ask the hotel manager (always deal with a manager) if you can have a block of rooms, a whole floor to yourselves, or a group discount. One bride I know managed to get her honeymoon suite for free with the six rooms she booked for her family. The guests paid for their own rooms, and she and her husband had a luxurious first night . . . on them!

People to find lodging for

| Out of town family | Groom's family | Groom | Bride (if necessary) |
| Groom's parents | Bridal party | Relatives | Friends |

One of the most important tasks you'll need to undertake before you book any rooms is making sure the hotel can meet your guests' specific needs. So when you find out that your guests want to book a room in town rather than drive home that night, keep this list handy for a "room interview."

1. Do you need a smoking or nonsmoking room?
2. Do you need a lower-floor room? (Some people are afraid of high-level rooms.)
3. Do you need handicapped access rooms?
4. Do you need a crib?
5. Do you need a cot?
6. Do you need an efficiency? (For longer stays, guests may wish to make coffee or breakfast on their own.)
7. Do you need double or king-size beds?
8. Do you need a coffeemaker in the room?

If you pick up the tab for your guests' lodging, be sure to make arrangements with the hotel manager that all of the guests' room service and phone call fees will be billed to them. If you pay for the room in advance, these charges will go to the guest. You might also ask to put a block on any adult channels for the rooms. You may not want your guests' kids tuning in during the late-night hours. If you can't do this ahead of time, tell the parents that there is this option.

Welcome Baskets for Guests' Rooms

It is a wonderful idea to have the hotel manager place a gift basket in the room of each of your guests. Some hotels have fruit baskets, cheese platters, and the like, but this is a chance for you to use your creativity and welcome your guests to the wedding celebration by giving them something to make them feel at home.

Shop at a craft store for as many pretty baskets as you need—one for each room is fine. If two couples will be sharing one room, obviously you will need to supply two. Fill the baskets with any selection of welcome gifts. Here are some ideas.

1. Sodas, fruit juices, bottled water, wine, liquors, beer
2. Bagels and muffins
3. Snacks and chips
4. Girl Scout cookies—a crowd-pleasing favorite!
5. Fruits, nuts, and Power Bars
6. Toys and games for the kids
7. Tourism books for the area, along with subway or bus tokens, gift certificates, and show tickets
8. Romantic baskets for couples—candles, massage oils, a bottle of champagne, two glasses . . .

Lodging Comparison Worksheet

Name _____

Address _____

Phone _____

Fax _____

E-mail and Web Site _____

Contact _____

Discounts/Package? _____

Included/Not Included? _____

Cost _____

Distance/Easy to Reach? _____

☐ Nonsmoking rooms

☐ Internal entrances

☐ Pool/health club

☐ Arcade for kids

☐ Adequate parking

☐ Safe area

☐ Cleanliness

☐ Helpful manager

☐ Block of rooms/group discount

13

Gift-Giving

NO DOUBT YOU WILL GIVE many gifts to the happy couple—engagement gifts, shower gifts, wedding gifts, perhaps a gift for the rehearsal or bridal brunch. When considering what to give, be sure to choose something that's not only useful, but something that will become special to them. Engraved picture frames become a permanent part of their homes. A blender will burn out in a few years and become garage sale material. You want your gift to last.

Gifts for the Happy Couple

Here are some ideas, ranging from the ultraextravagant to the sentimental.

Ultraextravagant

- Paying for the entire wedding itself
- Paying for the honeymoon
- The down payment for a house
- A new car

159

- Paying the balance of their college loans, giving them a fresh start
- Cash, stocks

Extravagant

- An entire china and crystal set
- Large appliances for a new home
- Couches, recliners
- Bedroom set
- Entertainment center with big-screen television, VCRs, CD player, DVD machine, and so forth
- Lingerie set and his-and-her robes from Victoria's Secret
- Gourmet food club for a year
- Maid service for a year
- Landscaping for their new home
- Home computer system
- Home security system
- Cash, stocks

Standard

- Items from the registry: appliances, linens, decor, and so on
- Champagnes and wines
- Gift certificates to their favorite stores
- Cash, stocks

Sentimental

- Framed photos of relatives
- Custom-made photo albums
- Edited videos of the couple through the years
- Handwritten notes from family members
- Heirloom jewelry and antiques that have been handed down through the generations

Of course, you know the couple. If they are kayaking freaks, you might get them their own boat. If they are sports fans, they may want season tickets for their favorite teams. If they love the theater, get them a selection of Broadway play tickets. The choice is entirely up to you, and the aim is to get them something that will take their breath away. Some more creative parents have given their kids vacations other than the honeymoon, such as ski trips, ballooning adventures, or dinner cruises. They have offered to pay for their car insurance for a few years as the kids struggle to get their careers in gear. Parents of couples who already expect their first child have given gift certificates for the design of the entire nursery. It's a completely individual choice. You know what they need and what they want, and you recognize that this is a once-in-a-lifetime gift-giving event, so make it special.

Gifts for the Bride

Some gifts will be for the bride herself. They may be shower gifts, a personal gift from you to her, even a little something for the bachelorette party. This is something you'll choose with only your little girl in mind, so put some thought into it, consider the ideas below, and get ready to spend some money on the bride.

- Her full trousseau
- Lingerie set from Victoria's Secret
- The wedding night peignoir
- Full service at a salon or day spa
- A week at a health spa
- A selection of her favorite books or music for her home
- Artwork
- A desk, computer, and other items necessary for her to start her own business
- Gift certificates to her favorite stores
- Framed photos

Gifts for the Attendants

When the bride asks you to help choose the gifts for her attendants, take the time to shop with her. Look through catalogs. Search for the perfect gifts. Here are some wonderful ideas to consider.

- Picture frames
- Eyeglass/sunglasses cases embroidered with the wedding date
- Photo albums
- Jewelry for the big day
- Framed favorite pictures of the bride and the attendant
- Aromatherapy products
- Candles
- Gift certificates to spas and salons
- Show tickets
- Gourmet samplers
- Beauty products

My mom called me from the mall to tell me about a big sale at a lingerie store there. I was able to purchase wonderful sachets, bath salts, lotions, and picture frames right then for my attendants. It turned into a fruitful shopping trip, and I put together gift baskets my girls loved. Thank God my mom called me for the sale!

—Ginger, bride

Whatever your choice, you can save a lot of time wrapping presents by buying gift bags and placing the items inside. This is particularly helpful if the girls will receive a selection of items, such as soaps, candles, beauty products, and the like. Gift stores can shrink-wrap baskets that you fill yourself; tied with a pretty bow, the presentation is lovely.

If you are called upon for gift ideas for the men in the bridal party, check out the items on the following list.

- Wallets or money clips
- Picture frames
- Colognes
- Flasks
- Watches
- Ties
- Gift certificates for sporting goods or clothing stores
- Gourmet samplers
- Show tickets
- Sporting events tickets

The groom, of course, is responsible for getting these items, although you may offer to help with selection and the wrapping.

Gifts for the Father of the Bride

He's been the forgotten man of the wedding planning process. He may have pitched in, doing his research, asking questions, and writing checks—as have you—but now he's facing a day that may be even more difficult for him than it is for you. Men, by nature, don't like to show their emotions very much, but inside he is melting over the fact that he's losing his little girl.

This is a nice time to show him how much you love him, how much he means to you, and what a great dad you think he's been over the years. Get him a gift that is special to him. It may be simply the perfect Hallmark card, saying "I Love You," or it may be something far more exotic, such as a weekend getaway while the kids are on their honeymoon.

Give it to him either at the rehearsal dinner or on the morning of the wedding, and you'll see that spark in his eye again.

Gifts for Your Other Kids

They've been left out of the action this past year, and while you were spread so thin with the wedding plans, you may not have given them all of the time and attention they wanted. But now is your time to make it up to them, thank them for their assistance, or even make them feel guilty for being such demanding, difficult little people (you are a mom, after all).

On the wedding day, you might give your other daughters jewelry, perhaps another heirloom piece from their grandmother. This inclusion will touch them and not make them feel like children.

Depending on their ages, you could present your kids with a gift certificate to a music or clothing store, passes to the cinema, even a promise of a day at the zoo . . . just the two of you. Dads can follow suit by taking the kids to a game, to a special event in town, or just out to eat by themselves.

Whatever your offering, make it special, and know that your child will forgive you for ignoring him or her. They may know how to make you feel guilty right back (they are your kids, after all), but they do love you, and they've missed your attention.

14

How's the Bride Doing?

THE DEEPER YOU GET into the process, the deeper the bride gets into her own emotions. You may find that she's stressed out, snapping at everyone, and just feeling miserable. You know enough not to blame it all on PMS, which her fiancé is likely to do, thus stressing her out all the more. You're the mom, and you know what it is. She's overwhelmed.

Again, your daughter is facing the pressure of planning the wedding of her dreams, watching everyone she knows running around to pull this day together for her, trying to keep her career or her studies running smoothly, trying to have something of a personal life, trying to please her future in-laws, and adapting to the very real notion of being someone's *wife* very soon. Her head is swimming.

She's been bombarded with a torrent of questions, she's had to make snap decisions, she's dealt with problems and miscommunications, she's been the target of everyone else's stress—which is not always handled very well—and somewhere in the middle of this she's supposed to be the radiant bride.

When your daughter rips your head off after you simply inform her that the seamstress appointment has been moved from 2 P.M. to 3 P.M., it's time to step back and remember what your little girl is going through. She is your daughter, and although she may be an adult, she probably still has a bit of that scared little girl inside of her, and it's coming out now. It happens to all of us once in a while. Your daughter has reached her boiling point, and—as always—it will be you she attacks.

You've handled her outbursts before. You know where she's coming from. Right now, even as your stress levels are high, it's very important to realize that your daughter means nothing personal by the words she says. She may accuse you of trying to run or ruin her wedding, even though you have no intention of doing so. If, indeed, you were a bit pushy, this is not the time to defend yourself. Just apologize, promise to watch yourself in the future, and give her the comfort she needs. Getting into an argument to assuage your own ego is the worst thing you can do.

All brides lash out at their mothers. There is always that big fight the week before the wedding when everyone argues and storms out of the house. Hours (or days) later, all is forgotten. Consider it a fundamental part of the wedding planning process. Nearly every bride I've spoken to said that it got to that point at some time. You may even remember fighting with your own mother before your wedding. If you can't remember now, it was probably so insignificant that you just didn't hang on to it.

Your daughter is most likely just venting her fears. This is a time of heightened sensitivity for her. Her fears may make her see sides of her fiancé that, right now, she doesn't like and is magnifying as some sort of sign that she's not supposed to marry him. His socks, left on the floor, have never bothered her before, but she's looking at them now as the *wife*. This is the kind of thing she's seen on television—as stereotypical wives arguing with their husbands. Every little thing is a big deal, and unless you step in and handle it the right way, the bride is likely to continue ranting and raving, and thus ruin the entire wedding experience—for herself.

That said, the most important thing for you to remember is this: Do not blame her, analyze her, or tell her that she's just stressed. The last thing she needs now is you criticizing her. Even if you're not actually criticizing her, she takes it as that. You have an intricate bond as mother and daughter. You know how to push each other's buttons without even meaning to. So the best approach is to take a totally new approach. Don't tell her to calm down and stop overanalyzing. That won't help. What will help is to give her what she needs: the opportunity to get it all out. To speak and not be judged. To hear herself verbalize the things that are going through her mind. She doesn't need you to tell her that what she's thinking is wrong. Once she gets it out of her head, she will hear herself, and she'll probably realize that it is wrong.

Your role in this wedding is to be her supporter, her cheerleader, her comforter. Take her out to lunch and promise that it is a non-wedding lunch. No talk of flower-girl dresses, menus, caterers, limos, or guest lists. No to-do lists, no time clocks, no appointments. It's just lunch. Go someplace nice where you can talk, just the two of you. It's a good idea to leave the groom out of this one, so she can be free to vent her fears about him as well.

If you make her comfortable and assure her that you're there to listen, she's likely to spill her guts to you. If you've never had a particularly close relationship, though, she probably won't divulge too much at this time, either. But maybe, in helping her, you can ask her older sister and lifelong confidante to do this job for you. This is not stepping aside and handing off the ball. It is doing what's best for the bride. Maybe, for some reason, she doesn't feel comfortable about being afraid to be a wife. After all, that is what you are, and she doesn't want to offend you. The poor bride is so afraid of offending people that she's miserable. So if you can't be the one to help her, find someone who will.

The best way to open any lines of communication is just to listen. Don't tell her what to do. As Mom, your immediate reaction will be to solve the problem. Just let her talk. If she asks for your advice, answer, with the caveat that that is just your opinion and it's ultimately her decision. Ask her what she's feeling. Ask her what makes her uncomfortable. Assure her that maybe it's not such a big deal, and remind her that the wedding itself is just one day. Remind her of the true meaning and purpose of it: not "everything has to be perfect," but "this is a celebration of our love and partnership." Sometimes she just needs to see things from a more relaxed perspective.

Don't be surprised if she still tells you that you're overstepping your boundaries. She may feel controlled by some of your decisions, even if she asked you to take care of certain matters. Many mothers of brides have sat slack-jawed as their daughters attacked them for taking over the wedding. "But you asked me to help!" is a statement not received well by the bride, who is lashing out in her helplessness. Your only recourse here is to avoid throwing a guilt trip, avoid backhanding an insult, and just think about it.

Have you overstepped your boundaries? Have you taken on additional jobs, telling the bride that you're just helping out because you have so much time, and you want to make it easy on her? If you've been *too* helpful, the bride may have agreed to your offers to help, just to be nice. In a short while, she began to feel resentful, and although she never said anything about it, she's taking it out on you now.

This is the time for you to honestly check yourself. Did you lapse into steamroller mode? If so, apologize. Tell your daughter that you didn't mean to offend her or to take any of the fun out of it for her. While you may not always do everything right, you had every intention of just helping.

It is very easy for you to get overexcited, overinvolved. Every mother of the bride does at some point. But if you consciously try to remember not to do that, you can stop that out-of-control train before it wrecks. You can get hold of yourself and put yourself at ease, and everyone else will be at ease as well. Sometimes your daughter may pick up on your increased stress level, and it will trigger her own. Your daughter is connected to you that way, so if you relax your tendencies to take everything so seriously, she will relax as well.

Perhaps the best way of helping your daughter is by helping yourself. Take some time to remove yourself from your role as Planner of the Wedding. Make it a smaller part of your identity right now. Give yourself back to other areas of your life—to the rest of your family, your hobbies, your job, your friendships, your husband. Practice stress-reduction methods such as taking a bath, walking every day after dinner, meditating, or listening to relaxing music. Few people in the world can go through a wedding planning process without becoming overwhelmed, especially when dealing with so many details, so you are not alone if you've lost the battle and become stressed. Just release it and start over with a calmer view.

Your daughter may follow your lead, taking walks, hanging out with friends more, taking baths, and getting away to pamper herself. And that will make her stronger and more able to handle the pressures ahead.

What If There's a Real Problem?

Though your efforts at reducing both your daughter's and your stress can help some-what, and the usual little blowups will occur over problems with the wedding, you cannot control what's going on with a bride who is having real difficulties.

While most wedding couples fight during the weeks before the wedding, it may seem odd to you that the bride and groom are fighting to a greater degree. It goes beyond their usual spats, and there is a sense that they are both fighting feelings of not wanting to get married anymore. This is a dicey road for you. Do you ask her if everything is okay? You can, but she may not answer honestly, since you and your husband have put so much effort and money into the wedding. Your daughter may not feel comfortable voicing her concerns to you. She may be swallowing her thoughts in an effort not to rock the boat.

Some mothers notice that their daughters are drinking more, acting withdrawn, or maybe sleeping too much. These are signs of depression, and your daughter should see a doctor.

Some mothers start to pry at this point. They may ask too many questions, become accusatory, and start voicing a dislike of the groom. The protective Mother Bear comes out, and it usually does not help the situation. What will help is being observant. Watch how the bride carries herself around her fiancé. Listen to how they speak to each other now. Has that changed? Beyond the fact that they are under pressure, does it seem that they resent each other? Indeed, the wedding stress may have them snapping at each other, but if their fights are more personal attacks, focus-ing on each other's weaknesses and name-calling, step in. Talk to the bride in calmer moments, and broach the subject by telling her about the time you had cold feet before the wedding, how you and her father fought, and how you were scared. Your daughter may open up.

I've spoken to many women who divorced shortly after marrying. Most of them said that inside they knew they didn't want to get married. Some knew as they were walking down the aisle but didn't say anything. Why? They didn't want to disappoint their parents. They knew a lot of money had been spent on the wedding, and they didn't want it to go to waste. This may seem outrageous to you, but it is so incredibly common. We don't all think rationally when we're under pressure, and the bride is certainly under enough pressure to turn a lump of coal into a diamond. The thought process isn't focusing on the right priority.

There are brides who do postpone or call off the wedding at the last moment, but the large majority go through with the wedding, stay married and miserable for years, and go through the pain and financial hardships of divorce. By this time, there may be children. A web of difficulties lies ahead.

This is not to say that this is your daughter's problem, but it may be. She may know in her heart that she doesn't want to get married. It may go way beyond the jitters, but she may not have the strength or knowledge to voice it. All of the divorced women I spoke to said they went through with it, even after voicing their fears to their mothers. Most of those moms just dismissed them, simply calling it cold feet and saying that they'd feel better once they get to the honeymoon. They didn't. Some couples fought *on* the honeymoon.

So if your daughter does get to the point that she says she's scared, that she doesn't know what she wants, that she wishes she could just run away and live in a lighthouse by herself, take it seriously. What you hear may be only a fraction of what she actually feels.

Do not tilt your head and make her feel like the little girl who wanted to quit Girl Scouts. This is marriage. It is serious. If your daughter is expressing serious concerns, you should take it seriously, too.

What do you do? Handle it carefully, and *keep her confidences.* The most important thing to her right now is the protection of her thoughts. If she confides in you, promise her that it will go no further. And make sure it doesn't. If you think your husband should know, ask the bride how she feels about bringing him in on the discussion. If she is against that, consider her decision gospel.

The next step should be getting her to voice exactly what she is upset about. While you may be the person she wants to talk to, it is a very good idea for you to suggest a counselor, a member of the clergy, or a therapist, who might know the ins and outs of psychology better than you do. A trained counselor knows how to get the patient to solve problems on her own. You are attached to the issue. Your daughter knows you are attached to the wedding. She may not be able to tell all to you.

In protecting her best interests, ask her if she would consider talking to a professional. Assure her that you always want to help her, but maybe she would feel better talking to some uninvolved third party. You know your daughter. You know what she would be comfortable with.

If your daughter does decide she wants to call off the wedding, know that this is a horribly difficult decision for her, and she wouldn't make it if she weren't entirely convinced that this is the right move for her. Though this is a financial and logistical nightmare, and it will tear the hearts out of at least a few people involved, it is her decision, and the best thing you can do is support her in whatever she wants to do. As difficult as this moment is, know that it is not nearly as difficult as divorce is.

If the wedding is called off, do the smart thing. Don't cancel everything and call everyone yet. Give it a while. Your daughter and her fiancé may be reeling. Their fight may take a while, but they may patch things up after a few weeks. So, if there is enough time to avoid losing deposits and the like, hold off on the sad string of phone calls.

The Basic Rules for Helping the Bride Through a Tough Time

Dos

- Do encourage her to take some time off and relax.
- Do get her out of the house to a neutral place where you can talk.
- Do encourage her to do most of the talking.
- Do tell her you'll support any of her decisions.
- Do tell her that the family will support her as well.
- Do tell her that you have faith in her, as she is a capable adult.
- Do tell her that while jitters are normal, more serious concerns require some action.
- Do tell her you won't be mad if she cancels.

Don'ts

- Don't trivialize her feelings.
- Don't tell her she's just nervous.
- Don't says she's never followed through on anything.
- Don't say, "But we spent so much money already!"
- Don't tell everyone she's scared.
- Don't hold a grudge against the groom. He's scared, too.
- Don't neglect any signs of her depression.
- Don't be judgmental or pushy.
- Don't make her feel like a failure.
- Don't try to talk her out of her decisions.

15

The Week Before the Wedding

THIS IS CRUNCH TIME, perhaps the period when you're most needed. All of the little details that couldn't be done ahead of time need to be taken care of now. All of the confirmations need to be made and the real choreography of the day takes shape right here. And, Mom, you're the ringmaster. Of course, the bride and groom are present, and they will take care of a great deal of the tasks, but you may find yourself in the position of checklist manager while everyone else attends to her or his own business.

Very often, the kind of problems that crop up during a wedding are a result of something that was forgotten the week before. So here is a list of all of the things that need to be done this week.

- ☐ Confirm with the officiant.
- ☐ Confirm with the ceremony musicians.
- ☐ Make sure the ceremony musicians are clear on which songs are to be played.
- ☐ Confirm with the limousine company.
- ☐ Make sure the limousine company has a detailed copy of the pickup/drop-off locations.

- [ ] Confirm with the florist.
- [ ] Make sure the florist is clear on what is to be delivered where.
- [ ] Confirm with the caterer.
- [ ] Give the caterer the final head count.
- [ ] Confirm with the photographer.
- [ ] Confirm with the videographer.
- [ ] Confirm with the DJ or band.
- [ ] Make sure the DJ or band is clear on the song list.
- [ ] Confirm with the baker.
- [ ] Confirm the tuxedo rentals.
- [ ] Contact any guests who have not responded for the wedding or the rehearsal.
- [ ] Confirm all details with the bridal party.
- [ ] Confirm all lodging and transportation for the bridal party, family, and guests.
- [ ] Make any last-minute adjustments to the seating chart.
- [ ] Using the seating chart, write out place cards.
- [ ] Finish making favors.
- [ ] Deliver favors to the banquet hall.
- [ ] Confirm with the banquet hall manager that all professionals can get into the banquet hall when they need to.
- [ ] Confirm the totals of final payments for all vendors.
- [ ] Write checks, or assemble cash, and place them in labeled envelopes for wedding day payment.
- [ ] Pick up the wedding gown and veil.
- [ ] Pick up shoes and accessories.
- [ ] Pick up the garter.
- [ ] Pick up the cake knife and server.
- [ ] Wrap and label bridal party gifts.
- [ ] Pick up tuxedos and shoes.
- [ ] Finalize plans for the rehearsal.
- [ ] Make bridal salon appointment.
- [ ] Make sure the men get haircuts now.

- [ ] Pack for the honeymoon.
- [ ] Confirm honeymoon reservations.
- [ ] Confirm the bride and groom's wedding night accommodations.

Be prepared for any number of unseen snafus. With so many plans in the works, it's only a matter of odds that something may get a bit off-kilter. Don't let it throw you. Just try to fix it, and if that is not possible, then try to arrange a suitable replacement.

16

The Twenty-Four-Hour Countdown

IN THIS LAST TWENTY-FOUR HOURS before the wedding, everything may seem like a blur. You're going in twenty different directions at once, everyone needs something from you, and your nerves are shot. Take a deep breath, slow down, and know that you've done a wonderful job so far. Everything is as much under control as it can be.

Remembering to keep the bride and groom calm, you can do your job with as much efficiency as possible. It just takes organization at this point, and your people-handling skills will be much in demand right now.

The Rehearsal

If nerves are going to start jangling anywhere, it's likely to be here. This is the first time the bride and groom will be walked through the ceremony, which will be performed *the next day*. It's the first time you'll see your daughter walked down the aisle, and it'll hit you, even though she's not in her gown.

You may think your job here is to sit in your front row seat and listen, but you may actually have to round up nervous, hyper wedding attendants and encourage everyone to take this seriously. Or you might be a part of the ceremony yourself, finding out now that the bride wishes to have you walk her down the aisle along with her father. You might be asked to light a candle, perform a reading, or even perform a song during the ceremony.

Whatever your role, you may be the only one with the presence of mind to ask the real questions. The bride and groom may have never done this before. They don't know what to ask. The bridal party may have done this a million times in other weddings, so they're not really paying much attention. The minister may gloss over details, as he knows what his own job is. But you will and should take it seriously—not so seriously as to be paranoid about every little detail, but seriously enough that people can be confident that everyone knows what he or she is doing.

Mother-of-the-Bride Tip

Make sure the marriage certificate is signed. Most officiants sign it during the rehearsal to avoid forgetting it the next day.

Even if the officiant wants to pack it in when you've only done one run-through, it can't hurt to suggest a second or third. Ask questions now, even if they don't pertain to you. So what if you come across as the nervous mother of the bride? That's what you are, and you'd rather have everything turn out all right than leave anything to chance.

The Rehearsal Dinner

Finally! A time to relax and unwind with the bride, the groom, the bridal party, and the groom's family. This is when you all get to take a breather, enjoy a nice dinner, and have some fun together. It may even be the first chance you all have to get to know one another, to discuss the things you all have in common, to begin your bond as extended family.

Tradition often says it's the groom's family's responsibility to plan and host the rehearsal dinner, but that, like everything else, is always up for consideration. The more you all attempt to do what's right for you, rather than what's prescribed in books, the better off everyone will be.

Regardless of who's paying, this is the time for making toasts, exchanging gifts, and videotaping everyone at play. Welcome the groom to the family. Tell the bride she's going to look beautiful and not to be nervous. Laugh about the little obstacles you've overcome up to this point. Relax, enjoy. This is where all the planning begins to pay off.

Tomorrow is the big day.

Before Midnight

Whatever your plans for the night before the wedding, be sure to separate the bride and groom before midnight. Tradition, and indeed superstition, declares that the bride and groom not see each other the morning of the wedding until she comes walking down the aisle. So allow them one last kiss good night and bring the bride home. They'll probably talk on the phone all night anyway.

Everyone will need a good night's sleep—or at least as much sleep as you'll be able to get, considering how nervous and excited you'll all be—so it's best to call it an early night. When you get the bride home, stay up a little while longer, though, so you and she can have some quiet time together to talk, to reassure her that everything will be fine, to get her to release her stress and know that everything is in place for her perfect day.

Some parents of brides choose this moment to give the bride a special gift just from the two of them. Some families watch old home movies together, order a pizza for a late-night snack, or even open a bottle of champagne for a midnight toast. This may be a very precious time for you, a moment you'll all be glad you took.

Be prepared to feel somewhat stressed the night before, as you realize the big event is so close. The realization that this is the last night your daughter will sleep in her bedroom as a single woman can be depressing, but you have to keep in mind that this is the happiest time in her life. So be happy for her.

—Joanne, mother of the bride

My last night at home was bittersweet. I sat up and talked with my parents, who have the best marriage I've ever seen. They gave me all kinds of really useful advice that I will remember forever. Even better, they said they're really happy I chose Evan to be my husband. He's the son they never had. I loved that.

—Heather, bride

17

The Wedding Morning

THERE WILL BE A SPLIT SECOND when you wake up this morning and it hits you: This is it. This is the big day. You'll probably have a flood of emotions that range from happiness to sadness, nervous jitters to relief. A mountain of must-do's may snap into your mind, and you may panic at the thought of all that has to be done. If you're this frazzled, imagine how the bride must feel. She's waking up knowing that her life will change forever on this day. If ever you're needed to pull it together and get the show on the road, it's now.

The mother of the bride shines in her role on the morning of the wedding. You'll share quiet private moments with your daughter, crack the whip and get everyone ready on time, choreograph and mobilize, then look dazzling for your departure. The bride is counting on you to run this whole morning without getting *her* ruffled in any way. Assure her that you'll take care of all of the little things, and that she's free to just relax and savor every moment of the getting-ready process.

Here's how to start: Make sure to provide a breakfast for everyone. Even if you just run to the local diner to get a pot of coffee, some juice, and a selection of bagels and muffins, it's your job to make sure people have something in their stomachs to make it through the morning. Many a bride has fainted due to lack of nourishment before the ceremony. So push those breakfast buns. And send a tray of breakfast foods over to where the groom and his ushers are readying themselves for the big event. They'll need food in their stomachs as well.

A nice touch before everyone actually starts getting dressed is to fire up the video camera and take some candid interviews. Ask the bride how she feels. Ask her what she's excited about. Ask her to talk about how much she loves her husband-to-be.

≈

One of the best parts of my wedding video is the footage we have of me right before I start to get ready. I look so nervous, but it's a good contrast to how I look after I'm all made up and in my gown. It's a great shot.

—Brianna, bride

≈

Interview the father of the bride. After the wedding, it will be funny for everyone to see him pacing, picking on the buffet snacks, even downing a quick drink before the day gets under way.

Interview the bride's brothers and sisters. Ask them how they feel. Ask them to send a message of their congratulations to the bridal couple. Do the same for the bridal party.

Have someone hold the camera so that you can give a little interview. Keep it short, though. You have a lot to do.

Get candid shots: the flower girl fussing as flowers are tucked into her braids, the bridesmaids comparing notes on run-proof stockings, the mother of the groom chatting with the bride. If all of the women are off to the salon to get their hair done, take the camera with you. It's a wonderful thing to capture the "transformations" of all of the women, to get before-and-after shots.

Think of this as capturing moments that the bride is too busy to appreciate. Later, she'll look back on this footage and be so grateful that you remembered to film it all.

This is not to say that you're to become a paparazzo! Just grab some quick shots and get back to the tasks at hand. There is a lot to be done. Perhaps calls need to be made. Late deliveries must be tracked down. Undoubtedly, the groom will call with any number of little difficulties, such as forgotten transportation for a family member.

The bride will be nervous, of course, so you might find it best to let her go about her own business and come to you if she needs you for anything. Although your nerves are up, don't transfer your stress onto her by reminding her every two minutes of something she hasn't yet done. She'll get to it. The best thing you can do for her is to relax, keep everyone else loose by being positive and cheery, and take care of actual problems as they arise. No need to lapse into "what ifs." What if the organist doesn't show up? What if the caterer forgets the appetizers? It's very easy for the nervous mind to imagine various mishaps, but you will enjoy the day much more if you let go, accept that some small things will go wrong, and remember you can handle whatever comes to pass. Your quiet confidence will relieve much of the bride's fear.

Let her get ready in peace. She'll need some time to herself this morning, so respect her wishes if she doesn't want anyone to help her get dressed. Many brides wish to have some quiet time by themselves in the bedroom. For some, the moment when they step in front of the mirror in their wedding gown is nearly a religious experience, not to be marred by a crowd of women poking, arranging the veil, tucking in straps, and so forth. If she wishes to have this moment alone, let her. It's the sanctuary she needs right now.

If she does invite you to help her dress, savor this special moment. It may hearken back to the days when you dressed her for her first day of school or helped her get her prom dress to fit just right. It's an emotional time for you, Mom, and you should appreciate that you're there to share it with her. She will look breathtaking when she slips that gown over her head and appears before you, as the bride, on her wedding day. A special moment is for you to place the headpiece on her head and secure it with pins. Watch out for this common mistake, though: Some mothers of brides are tempted at this point to pull the veil over the bride's face just to see what it will look like. Avoid this temptation, as you may very well get lipstick on the veil. Wait until she gets to the church to see that.

Dressing for the wedding is not always the most calm, serene time. Nervous, shaking hands wearing an engagement ring can snag stockings, so if you haven't thought ahead to buy a second pair, you may need to send someone to the store to buy the right replacement. Send the actual box of the old pair with that person, so that she buys the right size and color. Choose a reliable, calm helper for this job.

You might also ask the bride to step outside so you can check her makeup. Perhaps the lighting in the bathroom has always been terrible, and it is a good idea to see what her makeup looks like in natural light, especially if the wedding will be outdoors. Look for foundation lines by her jawline, and blend them in if it's a problem.

This time after dressing and before taking the photographs may also be when you and her bridesmaids bestow upon her the somethings old, new, borrowed, and blue.

❧

I gave my daughter a new and blue garter to wear. The old was my mother's handkerchief, and the borrowed were the pearls I wore at my own wedding. It was a special symbolic gesture for both of us.
—Renata, mother of the bride

❧

Take some time to think about the old, new, borrowed, blue. Remember that her maid of honor may wish to contribute something to this tradition, so call her the day before the wedding to check if she has any plans. (You don't want the bride standing there between you, in the awful position of having to reject someone's offer of new pearl earrings.) Again, get this moment on videotape if the videographer is not there to capture it.

In all things that morning, adhere to the bride's wishes. If she said that she doesn't want a circus atmosphere in the house, don't invite twenty relatives over for breakfast. Not only will that put the bride in the position of having to be sociable when she'd rather do deep breathing exercises, these twenty people won't see her in her gown for the first time as she walks up the aisle. Trust me, there will be enough chaos in the house that morning. Having to entertain guests will take away from your true role as hostess and helper for the day.

Have the photographer come over to the house really early, so that he can take his pre-wedding pictures of the women, the bride and her father, and of you and the bride at a slow and relaxed pace. You want the mood to be calm excitement, not "Oh-my-God-we-have-ten-minutes-to-get-these-shots!" If the photographer seems to be wrapping up this portion of the photos, don't be afraid to ask (nicely) for additional shots. Perhaps you want a candid shot of the bride and the bridesmaids out in the backyard. Perhaps you want a shot of the bride with her sisters only. Keep your mind clear at this point, think about what kind of shots you know the bride would love, but don't go overboard. Now is not the time to alienate the photographer. You want him to be receptive of your suggestions throughout the day, so make sure your requests are reasonable. Another thing to keep in mind: The photography package may include only so many rolls of film to be taken. Perhaps the photographer is saving more rolls for the ceremony and reception.

The closer it gets to the time that you leave for the church or synagogue, the higher the excitement level will rise. And so will the bride's nerves. Remember that the best way to keep her calm is to stay calm yourself. It will not make her feel better if you swoop down on her with many questions or tell her she looks pale. Just smile at her, give her a message of calmness through your eyes, and squeeze her hand to tell her she will be fine. Get her laughing, if you can. Reassure your daughter that she won't pass out if she just breathes and doesn't lock her knees. Tell the bridesmaids that they will look lovely, and give the father of the bride a reassuring kiss.

Then step back and look at the images before you as if they were a classic masterpiece of art. Take in the colors, the sights, the sounds, and memorize them. This is one of those priceless moments in life that will stay with you forever. As that cotton commercial says, "This is the good stuff."

18

The Ceremony

NO DOUBT YOUR HEART will be pounding when you pull up in front of the ceremony location. Keep in the forefront of your mind the only thing that matters right now: Your daughter and her true love will be married today. You look lovely and, most important, you're able to be there.

The attendants are busy with their own responsibilities now. The ushers are escorting the guests to their seats. The groom is no doubt pacing. The bridesmaids and maid of honor are keeping the bride—and her father!—calm. Now it's their turn to work and your turn to relax and enjoy the moment. The main part of your job as the bride's helper is finished. You've done a wonderful job. The plans are all laid for the unfolding of a beautiful day, and your daughter looks radiant.

This is the moment you've been waiting and planning for, the moment where you sit down and watch it all appear before you. So, as you're escorted to your seat (traditionally, you're the last person to be seated before the bridal procession begins), take a deep breath and smile. Everyone in that room is happy for you, and everyone is happy for your daughter and new son-in-law. Take in all the details. Remember the faces you see along the way.

All the months of planning come down to this moment. It's natural to be nervous, but just stay focused on the occasion. Nothing is as important as the vows.

—Joanne, mother of the bride

❧

The contents of the ceremony will have been explained in detail during the rehearsal. You know what's coming and when. Many parents will do more during the ceremony than just come down the aisle and sit through the service. Parents are reading passages, lighting candles, performing songs, and even giving witness. In some services, the bride and groom will come over to you and give you a kiss. Don't be nervous about whatever role you've been given in the ceremony. It'll be over in a flash, and the meaning of what you've done is far more important than the grace with which you've done it.

And in the end, when the ceremony is over and the newly united couple walk past you up the aisle, catch your daughter's eye and tell her you love her. She may be married now, but she'll always be your little girl.

The Receiving Line

Etiquette mavens like to prescribe a certain order that everyone must stand in, but the receiving line is completely up to the bride's and groom's wishes. I've seen beautiful weddings in which the bridal party and parents are lined up according to custom right outside the church. In order:

- Mother of the bride
- Father of the bride
- Mother of the groom
- Father of the groom

- The bride
- The groom
- The bridesmaids

I've also seen wonderful, fast-moving receiving lines made up of just the bride and groom and their parents. And I've seen couples hold off on their receiving line until the beginning of the reception, choosing instead to greet their guests as they enter the dining room from the cocktail party room. Talk with the bride beforehand to see what she wants to do.

Mother-of-the-Bride Hints

1. Give out breath mints to the bride, groom, and bridal party. Nervous breathing can cause bad breath. Take one yourself while you're at it.
2. If it's a hot day, arrange to have someone bring the bride and groom each a glass of ice water. All members of the receiving line may receive one as well.
3. Get pictures of the receiving line. It's a wonderful formation for those first just-married pictures.
4. Keep the guests moving along quickly, so that those still in the church waiting to move along the line don't have to wait long.
5. Introduce relatives from your family to the groom's parents, and they'll do the same.
6. Consider having champagne served at this point, depending on whether or not that's allowed at your location. Guests may be handed a champagne glass as they pass through the receiving line, and when the last guest goes through, a champagne toast is proposed.
7. Flower girls and ring bearers do not have to be included in the receiving line, although they might like to stand on the end to get their little dose of attention as well.

Another option, which has become popular these days, is to forgo the receiving line entirely. The bride and groom will just make it a point during the reception to visit each table of guests to receive their congratulations, and perhaps their wedding gifts. Since this has to be done anyway, many people consider a receiving line to be a waste of time, especially since the line may move slowly as chatty guests stop to have full conversations with the bride and groom. This option is more time efficient.

The Post-Ceremony Pictures

The newlyweds and their bridal party, along with the parents of bride and groom, often go to the bride's home or to a scenic park or garden for post-ceremony pictures. The vast majority of bridal parties do go to the bride's home, but you might choose one of the following options, if they're readily available to you, for a beautiful setting that will make the pictures lovely.

- A beach
- A fountain
- A waterfall
- A lake
- A mountain overlook

- A gazebo
- A garden
- A rose-covered trellis
- A merry-go-round

Whatever spot you choose as the setting and backdrop for the wedding portraits, it is very important to keep everyone organized, standing where they need to be, and ready for a quick succession of required and candid snapshots. Since everyone is in a rush to get to the cocktail hour or reception—if you haven't left hours between the events—you'll want to be sure that this process runs smoothly and that no one holds up the action.

Very often, the bridal party is relieved and excited, and a lot of mingling goes on between the ushers and bridesmaids. Here is where you have to crack the whip diplomatically, reminding them that there's a party to go to. You might choose to dangle the phrase "The sooner we get this done, the sooner we all get to party." Watch how fast they all take their positions.

Again, don't forget to recommend some shots to the photographer, but only after he's completed his lineup of standards. As you're suggesting shots, remember to ask the bride and groom if they'd like to have any special shots. While you're at it, ask the groom's family for ideas about portraits they'd like to have.

Don't forget some of the best candid photos for post-ceremony sessions.

- The flower girl playing in the garden
- The flower girl with the bride, sitting on the grass or on a boulder, by a fountain
- The bridal party jumping up in the air in celebration
- The bride and groom by the limo or Rolls Royce
- The bride's parents giving a high five
- Each set of parents alone
- The bride and groom with their brothers and sisters
- Favorite grandparents who have come along to be included in the shots

19

The Reception

AND NOW THE FUN OFFICIALLY BEGINS! The hard part is over, your daughter is married, and the celebration is on. Whether or not you've had a large part in planning the reception, you will fall into the role of official hostess. The guests will come to you as often as to the bride, saying how lovely everything looks, how beautiful you are, and what a wonderful wedding it was. You get to bask in the glow of the wedding without stealing any of the bride's spotlight.

Being the official hostess also means answering the caterer's questions (she may not want to hassle the bride about any number of little issues that may crop up during the party); helping an elderly relative to a better seat; and making sure the air-conditioning is on. Do not be surprised if you are repeatedly called upon to answer questions, to make decisions, and to take on the task of notifying the bride of a problem.

At one wedding, the cake topper fell off the cake. The mother of the bride thought it best to keep that fact from her daughter, who was busy mingling and having a great time. The mother's rationale was that the bride might get upset, and she didn't want anything to ruin her daughter's day. Though the cake topper was broken, and the top layer of the cake had smashed on the floor, the major catastrophe was hidden from the bride—even by the groom, who steered her gaze away from the area of cleanup—and a replacement cake layer was made. After the wedding, the bride was told about it and was angry that a secret had been kept from her—by her own husband, even. She was embarrassed that she was the only person in the room not to know. The mother of the bride could not possibly have expected this reaction. She thought she was doing the right thing at the time.

That said, it is your call whether or not to notify the bride of any problems. Small ones can be fixed without anyone knowing, but large ones may require notification. By all means, don't tell the bride about insignificant problems, such as two guests arguing over a business deal. She doesn't need to be let in on all of the human dramas that spring up whenever people of unlike minds gather together.

For most of the little problems, the manager of the banquet hall will be right there to help out. Having been in business for so long, and having planned many weddings, the manager will undoubtedly have an easy solution for most problems. They usually stock extra garters, extra throwaway bouquets, extra cake cutters, and so on, knowing that these things are often forgotten amid a mountain of more important details. So in the event of a forgotten item, ask the banquet manager first.

※

At my sister's wedding, I had to leave the reception, go home, and find her garter in her bedroom. While I was gone, I missed the conga line. The manager said he had an extra garter in his office, and I never had to leave.

—Karen, maid of honor

※

Knowing that all of the little intricacies and issues can be easily handled by the manager, yourself, the father of the bride, or even the groom, you can finally relax, dance, and have a good time. The vast majority of the day will go smoothly, and any little bumps that occur will have no weight in comparison to the beauty of the day and the fun all of the guests are having.

Modern weddings now incorporate special dances for all four parents, not just the father of the bride, so you may be able to arrange with the DJ or band ahead of time (they should call to ask your wishes and special requests, so mention this) for a dance that's special to you. Perhaps you can dance with your new son-in-law as well. For a fun touch, get the ushers out on the dance floor with you!

❧

The reception hours will fly by. Make sure you dance every song you can, dance with your husband, mingle and laugh, and take pictures. Leave the work to the professionals and have a good time. You've earned it.

—Joanne, mother of the bride

❧

A special touch suggested by many mothers of brides: Dedicate a song to your daughter. Just as you did at the engagement party, choose a special tune that reminds you of your little girl, and play it just for her. The bride and groom may love that idea and may dedicate a song back to you as well.

❧

My husband and I dedicated our parents' wedding songs to them. We had asked them ahead of time if they'd like that tribute as our thanks for helping with the wedding, and it turned out to be a good legacy-of-successful-marriages moment. It was very special to me.

—Danielle, bride

❧

We had set out a special display of silver-framed wedding portraits from both sets of parents, grandparents, and great-grandparents. Those in attendance were so excited to be remembered and included, and it was a nice way to include my departed grandmother in our day.

—Karen, bride

❧

Your Toast to the Happy Couple

This is the second of two times you have the spotlight at the reception. The first is your dance with your husband and the groom. Traditionally, the best man offers the first toast to the bride and groom. In most instances, his will be funny. If he goes for sentiment, however, by no means should you put pressure on yourself to do "better" than he does. Your toast should come later in the night, and it should contain words from your heart.

Many mothers and fathers of brides choose to propose a toast to their daughter and new husband, and the groom's family may also follow suit. Then, anyone else who'd like to lift a glass may do so afterward. Keep your toast short. The guests want to eat their dinners, dance, and celebrate, and your rambling monologue will only come off as an attempt to get some attention. So make it to-the-point. Remember, less is more.

If you're stuck on ideas for your reception toast, use these samplings from other mother-of-the-bride toasts to inspire your own ideas.

❧

I'd like to propose a toast to my daughter and her new husband. Never in my life have I been so proud of you, honey, and never have I been so proud to welcome into my family such a fine young man. We've watched your relationship bloom from the moment of your first date, and we are so happy that you've each found your soul mate. May God bless you both!

I'd like to propose a toast to the happy couple. Here's wishing you a lifetime of love, happiness, prosperity, luck, good health, and the opportunity to grow stronger and closer day after day.

I'd like to propose a toast to my daughter and son-in-law. If you bring one millionth of the joy to each other that you have brought to me over the years, you will be far happier than any human has a right to be. You are the lights of my life, and I love you very much.

The last year has been a busy one, and maybe I haven't taken the time to tell you how very special you are to me. So I'm taking the time now and joining my love for you with the love that everyone in this room has for you, and I hope you'll tuck it into your hearts always.

To my beautiful daughter and her handsome husband. . . . As you set off on your life together, know that you carry with you the love of your family, the best wishes of all who love you, and the strengths and grace that you have acquired on your own as you grew into the adults we are so proud of. They say that as parents, the best we can do is give our children roots and wings: roots to keep them connected to home and heart, and wings to fly off and succeed in their lives. So your roots are here with us, but your wings will take you anywhere you want to be. We love watching you fly.

Reception Tips From Mothers of Brides

It's fun time! For now, forget the problems, the missing matchbooks, the one missing centerpiece. You can deal with that later. In most cases, these little problems will be dealt with by the manager, and, if indeed no matchbooks had been ordered, you can negotiate the appropriate refund later. Now is not the time to be quibbling over $50.

Mingle as much as possible. Very often, distant family members only get together for these big events, and although you hate to think this way, it may be some of your elderly relatives' last big party. So spend as much time as possible visiting with guests, sitting down to talk, and complimenting them on their attire. In many families, weddings are the only time that visiting family members get to see one another, so this is a great opportunity to play catch-up and get the updates on everyone's lives.

Be sure the bride and groom remember to mingle. They may be caught up in the dancing, but you know they want to see and talk to all of their guests. So give a gentle reminder that the time between the first two courses is a great time for them to go see Aunt Lydia. Many brides, in looking back on their wedding day, say they wish they had had more time to speak with their guests. For the most part, older guests do leave early. Remind the bride of this so that she's not standing in a half-empty room at the end of the night, only then finding time to say hello to people.

Get the best pictures. If the photographer seems to be wandering around aimlessly or picking at the buffet after having taken all of the required shots, steer him toward some great shots that are developing before your eyes. Get the flower girl and ring bearer taking a tentative turn around the dance floor. Get the grandparents holding hands by the ice sculpture. Get a picture of your husband and his high school buddies—reunited for the first time in ten years. Get a shot of the great-uncles playing a card game at their table. Get a shot of the ushers smoking cigars by the bar. Supply each guest table with a throwaway camera for those fun candid shots. You never know what will be taken, and it is these fun shots that capture the moments the bride and groom miss as they're greeting guests, dancing, and staring into each other's eyes.

Mix up the music a little, but make sure the music fits the crowd. If you have primarily older guests, give them the big-band era music they love so much. Then, later in the evening when the younger set is still around, they can dance to their fast stuff. Include specialty songs, feel-good music, and any tunes you know your daughter and her husband like. For a fun part of the evening, encourage talented guests to perform a song themselves, serenading the couple.

Don't forget to incorporate your heritage. It's a nice touch of tradition to dance the tarantella or to play some ethnic music.

Be the guardian of the bride's and groom's gifts. If there's a gift table, keep it away from the exit doors and glance over at it occasionally for safe measure. If the bride and groom are handed primarily envelopes, have a special bag (I used the beaded bag my grandmother made for my mother's wedding) or box to put them all in. Perhaps a grandmother or relative who won't be out of her seat all night will help you play watchdog.

Bring an emergency bag to the reception! Fill a festive gift bag with such emergency items as these: painkillers, an extra set of pantyhose, lipstick, breath spray, emery boards, safety pins, sanitary napkins, additional film for your camera, contact lens solution, hard candies, insulin kits, and anything else you can think of. You'll be glad to have it stashed under your table when the items are needed.

Remember to eat. Too many mothers of brides busy themselves with the details of the reception, and especially with greeting guests, and they hardly take the time to sit down and enjoy the food that they all worked so hard to arrange. Don't worry about your diet, either. This is your daughter's wedding, so nothing has *any* calories! Sample everything you can, so you can get the full flavor of the day.

Make sure the bride and groom get to eat as well. Some brides and grooms miss most of the cocktail party if the photography takes too long after the ceremony. If this is the case, tell the banquet hall manager to leave the hors d'oeuvres out longer than planned so the bride and groom can taste the treats they've selected. If, during the night, you see the bride's and groom's dinner plates sitting at the table, unbeknownst to them as they're mingling with guests, tell them their dinner has been set out. You don't want them to eat a cold entrée or to miss their meal altogether in all the excitement.

Don't hassle the father of the bride if he gets a little bit drunk. This is his daughter's big day, and he's allowed. As long as he's not driving, there's no problem. Let him enjoy himself. The same goes for the bride and groom. Let them all deal with their hangovers on their own.

Watch out for jealous siblings. If the sister of the bride shows displeasure at being "a bridesmaid and not the bride," take her aside and tell her to stop being self-centered. Sometimes jealous siblings cast a shadow on the day by being visibly upset or withdrawn. Tell her to snap out of it and have a good time.

Get everyone on the dance floor. If younger guests are too shy to dance, ask them what songs would get them out there. It may be that the music just isn't right for them, so if you can get the DJ to play one song that they feel comfortable with, they may be more likely to stay out there. You might just need to get them started.

Fend off any criticism from judgmental relatives and friends. If someone is unhappy with the music or the selection of food, there's nothing you can do about it. And they're not the ones who have to be pleased with the day.

Be sure all guests have a safe ride home. Having a party bus or hotel shuttle available for transporting guests is a good idea, but if some guests who drove to the wedding are too drunk to drive home, insist on calling a cab. If they refuse, offer them a ride home at the end of the night.

After the Reception

The party is winding down now. The lights have come on brightly, and the guests are on their way out the door to head to their hotel rooms or back home.

If the bride and groom haven't left already, be sure to give them a special kiss good-bye and wish them well on their honeymoon. (Just be certain they have access to their luggage—is it in the car waiting for them or do they have to stop off at home? Do they have the keys? Their airline tickets? Their passports?)

The DJ or band will sense that the party's slowing down (or the clock has struck the end of the contract and they're packing up already), which usually makes the guests gather their favors and tell you what a lovely time they had.

This is a nice time to sit down with close relatives or friends and share some quiet moments in the nearly empty room. Savor the last minutes of the big event. You can look around with pride, knowing that the wedding was a big success. Everyone had a good time. The small crises were averted. The bride and groom wore smiles all night and danced on air.

❧

My husband and I asked the DJ to play one last song for us, and we danced alone in the room, closing down the party. It was pretty emotional, but we shared a special moment.

—Anne, mother of the bride

❧

Before you leave, search the room for items left behind by your guests or the bride and groom. Gather up the bride and groom's gifts and transport them to the location you've arranged with the bride and groom beforehand, whether it be your house, their house, or a friend's house. Perhaps an usher can help you carry them out to the car.

Before you leave, you will most likely have to settle up with the banquet hall manager. You may choose to do this now: to take care of final payments, tipping, and the negotiation for discounts for forgotten or unacceptable items. This is the norm, but some parents wisely choose to take care of all matters beyond handing over the check the next day. After all, you are tired, perhaps a bit drunk, and any kind of businesslike discussion would not go well in this state, especially if you have major gripes to air with the manager. Just tell him you will be in touch. You want to enjoy the rest of the evening.

At this point, you might choose to host a small gathering at your home. Invite the bridal party and some special relatives back to the house to end the evening with an intimate dessert-and-coffee party. This gathering should be relaxed and informal. You might all want to change into more comfortable clothes, getting out of those itchy tuxes and constricting stockings and sliding into jeans. Spend the time relaxing, talking about the elements of the day, and relishing the many, many compliments you receive.

Since you've all eaten so much at the wedding, you might simply serve some snacks, such as cheese platters, fruit salad, even sorbet or ice cream. Coffee may be poured all around, or you may have yet another champagne toast.

If, however, the house is in a state of disarray from twelve hurried bridesmaids getting ready that morning, you might decide to invite your special guests out to a lounge for a few more drinks. Some of the major hotel chains have piano bars and elegant lounges. Perhaps you might join your guests back at their hotel for a drink.

Whatever you do, it is a wonderful idea to wind the night down with relaxing time spent with all of your favorite people.

At the end of the evening, hug your husband and thank him for all he did to help plan this wonderful day. Thank your other children for their support, and get some sleep. You've earned it.

20

The Aftermath

ONE THING YOU MIGHT NOTICE after the wedding, or even the next day, is a big energy drain. All of the effort you put into the wedding is over now. It may have taken up a great deal of your time this past year, but now, with the wedding over, you have nothing else to think about. Many mothers of brides discuss this post-wedding letdown. The emotion you felt at the wedding has pulled everything out of you, and now you're left wandering around the house with nothing to do. Many moms say they've gone into their daughter's childhood bedroom, and the emptiness can be quite depressing. You've just been through an ordeal, and sometimes even the most joyous occasion can have its downside. But instead of missing your daughter, and missing the feeling of being involved in the wedding, know that there is so much more joy to come. Your daughter and her husband may buy their first home, have their first child, or experience the thrills of career success. You will still be there to celebrate those times, even if your daughter no longer lives under your roof.

So don't be surprised if you feel a little down or lethargic the day after the wedding. That's normal. Just get through it the best you can, find something else to keep yourself busy, and focus on all the positive aspects of what you have accomplished. You have just given your daughter the wedding of her dreams. You should be so proud of her and of yourself. Your bond as mother and daughter was not severed. In sharing this event, it has been made stronger.

For Their Honeymoon

There are lots of special things you can do to make the honeymoon more enjoyable than it's already likely to be. Here are some things other parents of brides and grooms have done to welcome the happy couple to their getaway:

- Have a bottle of champagne or a tropical fruit platter delivered to their room as a surprise.
- Have an area musician serenade them in their room. If they are in Mexico, arrange to have a mariachi band play outside their window.
- If you haven't picked up the bill for the honeymoon, pick up the bill for a gourmet dinner sent to their room the first night.
- Have the maid put rose petals on the bed.
- Send a snack basket filled with their favorite pickings for those late-night munchies. The mini-bar is way too expensive.
- Sneak a bottle of bubble bath or massage oil into the bride's luggage. (Just put them in a plastic bag so they don't leak!) Add scented candles and a CD of romantic music.
- For fun, add a note saying, "Don't do anything I wouldn't do!" On second thought, that could drive your daughter—or your son-in-law—into therapy! Better skip it.

While the Newlyweds Are Gone

It's sad, but criminal minds use wedding announcements to target empty homes for burglaries. So while the bride and groom are away on their honeymoon, make sure their place has at least the appearance of being occupied. It's a wise idea to have someone stay at the bride and groom's place or just to stop in every day to take in the paper and the mail, turn on lights, open shades, feed pets, and water plants. The newlyweds will be glad to know their home is taken care of and that there is nothing to worry about on the domestic front while they enjoy their getaway.

Another smart option, something most brides and grooms do not think about on their own, is to have their calls forwarded to your phone. Many voice mail systems and answering machines fill up quickly over the course of a few days, and the couple may not want to miss important business or personal calls. So discuss this option with them, see if they'd like you to take messages, and arrange with the phone company for a temporary rerouting of their calls.

What happens if an emergency arises while they are away? If it is a dire family emergency, such as a death, accident, or illness, and the couple absolutely needs to be notified, give them a call at their hotel to let them know. If, in the case of international travel, you don't know where they are, the Red Cross can help find them if it is seriously necessary.

Of course, this will take some serious thought on your part. Do they, after all, really need to know? Is it something that they can be told when they get back? For most mothers of brides, the choice is easy. They allow the couple to enjoy the honeymoon, and they let them know about a family member's accident or illness upon the couple's return. If, however, it is a case of the bride's father having a heart attack, the death of a family member, or some equally grim occurrence, the bride and groom should be summoned back. Always make sure it is a case of life or death, and that you are not just following your old habit of calling your daughter with every little thing. If they don't need to know, leave them alone.

They're Back!

When the newlyweds return home from their honeymoon, you can welcome them back in any number of special ways. A nice tip suggested by several moms: Fill the newlyweds' refrigerator with trays of food, casseroles, and favorite homemade meals.

They'll be glad to find that they don't have to cook when they arrive home from vacation—you know they'll have other things on their mind anyway. You're saving them from pizza delivery.

It might also be a nice touch to set out some fresh flowers on their table or a display of their gifts. Perhaps some of the pictures you've taken have come back from the lab. Leave them there for the newlyweds to see; they'll be anxious to look at any footage of their day. Or perhaps you could set out flowers and champagne by their bedside, along with a big basket filled with their favorite snacks, such as bagged chips, home-baked cookies, fruit snacks, nuts, candy bars, and the like. You might have their dog or cat bathed and groomed for them, tying a big bow around his or her neck.

If it is a lovely spring day, go to their place early and open the windows to get that fresh air scent in the house. Just be sure to stay at their place so no burglars get in. Open all the curtains, let the sunshine in, and place some potpourri around the house. Put fresh, clean sheets on their bed. They have, after all, just come home from a vacation during which they probably had fresh, clean sheets every day. And who knows how long it's been since the last time they did laundry! Just this once, it's nice to pamper them.

If the wedding video has come in (which is unlikely, but you may have some footage that other guests have given you), pop it into the machine, and display a note that says to push the PLAY button. The newlyweds will love to get their first glimpse of themselves and all their loved ones on their wedding day.

A Welcome-Back Party

Although they may want to be alone for the first couple of days, an informal gathering with the family and bridal party to watch the wedding video is always a fun idea. Invite the bride and groom's closest friends and family for a brunch or luncheon at the bride and groom's house. Set up a buffet or set out pretty trays of cold cheese and crackers, shrimp cocktail, and other hors d'oeuvres for easy picking for your guests—no slaving over a hot stove for you. Select an assortment of pastries or desserts, and serve mimosas for a classy champagne toast to the couple upon their return.

This is also a good time to give them a welcome-home present. Here are some of the better ideas I've heard.

- A mailbox with their married names on it
- A doormat with the same
- His-and-her robes (if they haven't received that as a shower gift)
- Family letterhead
- Address labels
- A filled-in family tree
- Anything that says you're a family now

And now that the wedding hoopla is over, you can start bugging them about giving you a grandchild. But that's another book.

Part Two

Wedding Planning Tools, Tips, and Tales

21

*Top Ways Moms Are
Helping With the Wedding Plans*

WEDDING PLANNING HAS GOTTEN FABULOUS again for the mother of the bride. After going through a few years of being bumped out of the wedding plans by wedding couples who opted to handle everything themselves (no matter who was paying), moms have been invited back into the VIP wedding planning team. Those wedding couples realized that missing out on planning with Mom was something they'd regret for a long time, and Moms bring fantastic skills to the table.

Here are the top ways that today's modern mom is helping with the wedding plans:

- *Tapping into their network.* Moms know people, and those people—like caterers, hotel managers, floral designers, and graphic designers—can offer up a friends-and-family discount, and bring top quality service and huge talent to the wedding details.

- *Using their career skills.* Moms with legal backgrounds review those vendor and site contracts to spot any bad terms and hidden fees. Moms with financial backgrounds can help create a viable budget. Moms with fashion backgrounds can open doors at top designer showrooms. No matter what your career skills are, you can help get the wedding couple huge advantages and big protection.
- *Planning parties.* From engagement parties to the bridal shower, the rehearsal dinner (yes, the mother of the bride might get to plan that one!) to the morning-after breakfast, moms bring their party ideas to life in the couple's honor.
- *Attend the bride's gown-shopping expeditions.* If you're in town, you may be invited to share your opinions on each dress, and sharing this dream shopping experience creates precious memories.
- *Tour sites.* You're an extra set of eyes assessing locations, perhaps asking the perfect questions of the site manager to save the day, or help the couple decide on the perfect setting.
- *Attend tastings.* Of wedding catering and cake samples in this fun group outing.
- *Find or make décor items.* You might have a great décor piece in the family, or go scouting for great pieces at estate sales, flea markets and consignment shops. Or, you might DIY décor pieces to add the couple's custom ideas to them.
- *Guest list etiquette.* You know who a cousin is married to, and you have their current address to help the wedding couple make invitation addressing easier.
- *Ritual expert.* If the wedding couple wants to include a religious or cultural ritual to their ceremony, they can consult you for the details and meanings.
- *Dress styling.* Of course, you're going to select the perfect, most stylish dress to wear on the wedding day, suiting the formality level and feeling your best on the big day.

- *Foodie pro.* If you're quite the chef, you can help the couple create the perfect wedding menu, and suggest theme and specialty menus for other celebrations.
- *Mobilizer.* If guests haven't responded by the RSVP date, you can take on the daunting task of calling those late people to ask for their decision. This is a task that some wedding couples like to avoid, and you carry authority to get answers.
- *Photo and video finder.* You'll go through your collection of your kids' photos and videos to find the perfect images and footage for the couple's montage, as well as photos for the family photo table.
- *Doing the fun stuff.* You might write to the Duke and Duchess of Cambridge, and baby George, to request a "Congratulations on Your Wedding" card from the palace, a delightful surprise for your Kate-obsessed daughter.

22

Top Ways to Plan on a Budget

As a planning partner, you'll rack up some expenses of your own, and you may also be entrusted with arrangements for the wedding day. You'll of course want to plan on a budget, without sacrificing quality or having any regrets later, so here are some top budget-planning tips:

- *Plan your party in the off-season.* The wedding couple might have set a wedding date for peak season when vendors and sites charge higher fees, but your party can take place during your region's off-season time when lower prices are everywhere.
- *Plan for a weekday.* A party on a Thursday night can cost 25 percent less than a party held on an in-demand weekend date.
- *Think about brunch.* A hotel's brunch might cost $25 per person for a huge catering spread, endless desserts and a free glass of champagne. A rehearsal dinner could, then, be replaced by a far less expensive and guest-pleasing engagement brunch.
- *Get on mailing lists.* And click Like on restaurants', dress shops' and other establishments' Facebook pages to get early notice of sales, "friend" discounts and other big-savings opportunities.

- *Coupon.* Learn how to use smartphone couponing, which is growing in popularity and outpacing print coupons. You always have your phone with you, so you always have access to potentially big savings. Add in coupons to craft stores, asking friends and family if you can have theirs as well, and you can get 60 percent off your total purchases, 2-for-1 deals and other price-slashes and freebies.
- *Freecycle.* Check out Freecycle.com to see if you can trade something you own, or a service you provide (like graphic design) to get something in trade for the wedding.
- *Ask friends if you can have their leftover craft supplies.* Everyone has bins of their kids' craft project supplies, and many people buy cake decorating kits and other craft store goodies on a whim, thinking they'll enjoy the hobby. But more often than not, those beads, cake pans, glitter markers, embossing sets, stamps and other items wind up in storage. If friends would like to declutter their basements, you might receive valuable DIY supplies for wedding projects.
- *Go to the copy shop.* Computer ink is pricy, and an invitation or program design with lots of color is going to use a lot of it. So check into printing out one program and then taking it to your office supply store for a more economical bulk printing.
- *Don't use square envelopes for invitations.* They cost more to mail.
- *Look into discounted gift cards.* Check GiftCardGranny.com to buy discounted gift cards that you can use at full value at the supermarket, department store and other locations for wedding items.
- *Go in-season with foods and flowers.* When they're in-season, they'll cost less. Your supermarket butcher and fishmonger can tell you what's plentiful and well-priced in-season.
- *Shop flea markets.* You could get a case of mason jars for a very low price, as well as other décor items for less.
- *Follow @weddingfreebies on Twitter* to potentially snag some terrific brand freebies and sweepstakes prizes.

23

Mom's Planning Timeline

You'll of course proceed at a pace set by the bride, and it might start way in advance of the wedding, or launch at full-throttle when a near wedding date is set. Use this timeline to help you plan your tasks, and personalize it to your own to-do list:

As Soon as Possible

Announce the engagement, with the wedding couple's blessing and via their requested method. They might want you to hold off on going to Facebook until they can call special relatives themselves.

Decide on what you can contribute financially for the wedding, and contact the wedding couple to offer your contribution.

Meet with the couple to talk about how formal or informal, and how large or small, the wedding will be, as well as if they want an engagement party.

Ask what they'd like you to work on for and with them before you take it upon yourself to start making plans.

If invited to participate, submit to the wedding couple your preliminary guest list names. When the couple finalizes their guest list, *then* you can start planning the engagement party.

Start planning the engagement party, which can happen as soon as the couple wishes.

Start asking friends and family for vendor recommendations.

Stock up on organization supplies.

Attend site scouting trips with the couple, if invited.

Nine Months Prior to the Wedding

Start shopping for your dress. Special orders at a bridal shop can take months to come in, and then they need to be altered.

Notify the mother of the groom about your dress choice once you've made your purchase.

Six Months Prior

Review vendor options and finalize contracts.

Book lodging for yourself and help out-of-towners with their lodging plans.

Start working with hairstylist in order to find the best look for the wedding.

Make your wedding-day beauty appointments.

Attend menu tastings and cake tastings with the couple.

Four Months Prior

Order invitations for events you'll host.

Contact the maid of honor to offer your assistance with the bridal shower, if needed.

Work with the bridesmaid group on the bridal shower plans.

Begin planning the morning-after breakfast.

Help to plan seating charts for the reception.

Assist with your husband's tuxedo rental, if needed.

Assist your other children with their wedding day wardrobes if not in the bridal party.

Two Months to Six Weeks Prior

Confirm hotel room block for out-of-town guests.

Mail your event invitations.

Attend dress alteration appointments.

Buy wedding day shoes and accessories.

Finalize plans for DIY projects you'll be working on.

Four Weeks Prior

Help to finalize seating charts as acceptances and regrets come in.

Complete DIY projects.

One to Two Weeks Prior

Contact guests who haven't responded to invitations.

Call and confirm dates and times with vendors.

Make your wedding-day checklist.

Tie up any loose ends.

One Day Prior

Attend rehearsal and rehearsal dinner.

Assign last-minute duties to friends and family members.

Get a good night's sleep.

Charge your cell phone and camera.

Confirm your limousine reservations, if needed.

24

∿

Top Wedding Experts' Tips for Moms

THE FIRST RULE OF DRESSING when you are a Mother of the Bride (MOB) is that you are *not* the bride. It is not your day, even if you are paying for the whole thing. The focus should be on your daughter. Now that said you still want to look fabulous! Here are some of my top tips for mother-of-the-bride style on the big day:

Ceremony

- Consider not just the formality of the wedding, but also the time of day and the style of the venue, so that you look lovely in that setting.
- Ask your daughter what she would like you to wear. Some brides like the MOB to coordinate with the wedding colors, and others do not.
- Consider the color scheme of the wedding. If the bride does not have a specific color she wants you to wear, then do not try and match the bridesmaids. But you will want to coordinate with the

color scheme and the season. A MOB should never wear a loud or over the top color such as bright orange.

- The length of the MOB dress should match the length of the bridesmaids' dresses.

Brunch and Rehearsal

- If the MOB is hosting either event, she should lean toward the dressier side.
- Venue is a huge consideration: is the event outdoors? Formal sit-down dinner? Picnic? Dress for comfort and style in your venue, especially if you will be outdoors. Make sure your dress will not be too sheer in outdoor sun, for instance, and that a breezy venue won't have your dress skirt flying up.

—Keylee Sanders, celebrity stylist and owner of Style Studio, KeyleeSanders.com; @KeyleeStyle

I tell all my clients to find the strengths and make a fun project out of it. If the mother has excellent taste in fashion or food décor, then incorporate them in your shopping, floral appointments, tastings. Or, join in on the cake tasting or a wine and cocktail tasting. For my own wedding, I knew how much my mother-in-law loved making wine. My fiancé now husband and I decided to ask her if she would enjoy making a special wine for our favors. She was thrilled and our guests were too! We also knew both of our mothers enjoyed and were good at card making. Since we were having an intimate wedding of 50 guests we thought it would be fun to do our wedding invites and paper items. We made it a family weekend with our moms and dads, and made very detailed, elaborate invites. It took us about 26–30 hours but we were all together having fun. I would not recommend making invites if your guest count is over 50 people.

—Courtney Kern, founder of Events Beyond

The trend I'm seeing lately is that most couples are paying for their own weddings so the mother of the bride takes a little bit of a backseat in the planning process.

They participate more in a consulting role, offering their opinion on a variety of subjects. Looking at ceremony music, there's a number of mothers who assume that their daughters know little about music and try to choose the selections without consulting them. No matter how much a mother says, "Oh, my daughter trusts me completely when it comes to ceremony music," I always get the okay from the bride as well, just to make sure they're getting what they want. It is their day after all.

—*Yury Shubov, president of Ideal Ensembles*

Choose a location with a terrific historic background, a "story" that guests will enjoy while they're staying in the hotel or enjoying the ballroom. Our hotel used to be a convent many years ago, and our ballroom still has many of the convent's chapel details. Now, guests dance and celebrate in what used to be a chapel, which makes the event even more interesting to them.

—*Ruben Alvarez, director of sales at El Convento Hotel in Old San Juan, Puerto Rico*

What's popular for party fare now is "light bites," delicious gourmet bite-sized finger food rather than a big spread of foods that can seem wasteful to guests. For instance, many wedding hosts are mindful not to serve too many carbs, so that big pasta station may be eliminated in favor of fresher, crunchier, locally-sourced foods. It's still creative food. It's just not a *ton* of food.

—*Marie Danielle Vil-Young, celebrity wedding coordinator at A Votre Service Events*

Marie Danielle says that after the wedding, she remains friends with many of the mothers of her upscale clientele. They establish a warm and respectful relationship, and she says that the moms are "beautiful, elegant, fashion-forward, very educated, and powerful—and they know it, but they are not pushy and are happy to step aside to let the bride shine."

25

Top Etiquette Tips
for Moms

ETIQUETTE IS SO IMPORTANT for weddings, and moms often set the standards for proper behavior and consideration. Even though etiquette rules have bent in today's weddings to some degree, there are still important rules for moms to keep in mind:

Invitations

- Never mention the wedding to *anyone* before the bride and groom have finalized their wedding guest list. You don't want to disappoint anyone you may have told when they don't make the final guest list.
- Provide the wedding couple with family members' and friends' full names, titles, spouses', partners', and kids' names and addresses, so that they can use good etiquette in addressing their invitations.
- Only guests invited to the wedding get invited to an engagement party or the bridal shower.

- Not all wedding guests have to be invited to the bridal shower. It's okay to create a guest list of just the closest family members and friends.
- Ask the wedding couple how they feel about e-invitations. They're more acceptable for wedding invitations than ever before, and for engagement parties and bridal showers, they're etiquette-okay. But the wedding couple makes the final decision on that.
- If you're invited into the bridal shower group planning the bridal party, you're to be named as a co-host, not as the main host, no matter what you're paying.

Your Dress

- Ask the bride for input on which colors you shouldn't wear. While it's long been an etiquette rule that no one wears white but the bride, and that black means "mourning," many brides now want all their guests in white or black.
- Ask the bride for input on your dress style and color before you shop. She may have a vision for you, and coordination plan for the moms.
- You don't have to match colors with the mother of the groom. You choose your dress first, and she chooses a complimentary style and color.
- You don't have to match dress colors with the bridesmaids.
- Old etiquette rules said not to dress too flashy, but today's moms are comfortable with some sparkle and showing some skin. Show your dress prospects to the bride to get a feel for her comfort with your stand-out style.

Social Media

- Don't post on your Facebook page or other social media platforms any details about the wedding without the bride's okay. She might not want you ruining surprises or stealing her thunder.
- No thinly-veiled complaints or venting about the wedding plans on your social media pages.

- Befriend the mother of the groom on social media, to form a connection and build a relationship. You may be planning wedding details with her, and you'll be a part of each other's lives in the future.

After the Wedding

- Send a note of happiness to the groom's family, telling them how great they looked on the wedding day and how happy you are to be an extended family with them.
- Send thank-you notes to anyone who helped you with your own wedding details, including your beauty stylists and helpful friends and family.
- Send a thank-you note to the wedding couple, thanking them for welcoming you into the wedding planning circle, and telling them how much you love them.

26

Top Roles for Moms in Bridal Shower Planning

MORE MOMS ARE BEING INVITED TO JOIN in the plans and hosting of the bridal shower these days. Moms love it, because they get the fun of planning, and bridesmaids love it, because moms help with the costs and help with the legwork. Brides love it because their moms get a fun task to join in on. Everyone wins.

Here are some of the top roles that moms take on for the bridal shower:

- *Helping with the guest list*. Providing names of essential relatives to add to the list, and providing addresses for invitations.
- *Choosing the place*. Moms may tour sites with the bridesmaids, or know the perfect restaurant for the party setting.
- *Allowing the party to take place at their home.*
- *Adding to the budget*. And perhaps taking on the cost of special, added items like a dessert bar in addition to the cake.

221

- *Menu and cake selection.*
- *Décor plans,* including getting décor items and setting up.
- Making favors. They could be baked, frosted cookies or brownies, from mom's own recipes, or personalizing store-bought items.
- *Arranging a photo display.* Of the bride through the years, or of the couple during their courtship.
- *Arranging the surprise.* If it is one, she may be the ringleader in throwing the bride off-track and then having her brought to the party.

When planning with the bridesmaids, be careful not to get overly excited and step on the maid of honor's toes, steamrolling your ideas and frustrating everyone. Bridesmaids often complain that the mom wants an old-fashioned game played at the shower, and forced that into play, for instance. Just ask what you can do to help, and enjoy being part of the planning team.

27

Top Roles for Moms in Destination Wedding Planning

DESTINATION WEDDINGS ARE BECOMING MORE POPULAR, whether it's a wedding taking place on a far-away tropical island, overseas in an exotic city, or just a few hours away from your hometown at a family resort, beach or ski town. No matter the destination type, the fact remains: you may be helping to plan a wedding that takes place at a distance. And that distance introduces a few extra steps and tasks that may be your assigned responsibility.

Here are some of the top roles that moms are taking on for destination weddings:

- *Spending time helping to research the destinations themselves,* such as finding the top-rated resorts on a particular island, reading those resorts' online reviews, and contacting the wedding planners at the resorts to have their wedding brochures and intake forms sent to you. It's a big world out there, so your many hours of research can go a long way to helping the wedding couple narrow the field . . . and you may just be the one to find their dream resort or exotic city's luxury hotel.

• *Researching discount travel options.* In addition to the usual travel websites you might use often, like Kayak.com or other pricing sites, you may also check with destination wedding resorts to see what their wedding packages include, such as airfare, boat transfers to the resort (some are included, and some are pricy!), car rentals and more.

• *Researching options like booking a villa* at the resort so that everyone can stay together in a fine home with private pool and private beach, if the price and experience are better than having everyone stay in rooms at the hotel.

• *Fielding destination wedding guests' questions* about the resort, hotel room bookings, travel details and perhaps even letting guests know about group airfare discounts you've found. Some airlines offer group discounts especially for destination weddings, and some of these include discounts on car rentals for your guests. You could save everyone hundreds of dollars, including yourself!

• *Paying for and hosting the welcome cocktail party.* At an island resort, that might be a private dinner on the beach, with a bonfire and steel drum music, just for the destination wedding guests. At a family resort one state away, you might book your party for poolside or for a private party room or atrium. You may wish to take on this extra party, so that guests who are traveling quite a distance arrive to a terrific celebration.

• *Planning a destination wedding weekend group activity,* such as a morning catamaran sail with snorkeling in a gorgeous cove, or a guided bus tour of the island's historic sites, or a winery tour in wine country, a tour of a brewery, or a scheduled His Side vs. Her Side sporting event.

• *Spreading the word about the couple's honeymoon registry.* They'll have a link to it on their personal wedding website (and if they don't, encourage them to do so), but you can also let guests know about it via old-school word-of-mouth or inserts in the bridal shower invitation.

- *Shipping wedding items to the resort ahead of time.* Those favors, décor items and other wedding items will be too bulky and too expensive to bring with you on the plane, so you can take on the task of shipping supplies to the hotel, insured and trackable, and of course in advance to arrive there in time.
- *Acting as packing guru.* You can take the lead in packing any essentials such as important paperwork, and light wedding supplies that can go in your suitcase or carry-on. (License papers should stay with you!) And you may also be the one entrusted with packing up the wedding gown in a garment bag so that it stays relatively wrinkle-free and bringing it with you on the plane. This is precious cargo, so watch after it and keep it safe delivering it to the bride.
- *Making guest welcome baskets.* If assigned, you'll select the items to be included in guest welcome baskets, awaiting them in their rooms when they check in. You can pack and bring the bags and lots of little gift items, or arrange with your resort to have items provided. You might also bring the gift bags or totes with you, and shop in the hotel gift shop for the guests' goodies, then insert the bride and groom's hand-written thank you notes in each bag, and arrange delivery of the bags through the hotel concierge.
- *Arriving the day before to organize everything.*
- *Being chief mingler.* As host of the welcome party, or just in your esteemed role as mother of the bride, you'll mingle with guests on both sides of the family. To make introductions and put everyone at ease, let everyone know you're the point person if they have any questions, and also let guests know the name of the wedding coordinator or resort's concierge if they should need anything.
- *Participating in the wedding.* You might play a part in the local culture's wedding ritual, such as handing a symbolic item to the bride and groom, or you might simply dance a special dance at the reception. You're a full participant to make the wedding even more meaningful and fun for the wedding couple and the guests.

28

New Trends in Mom-Hosted Parties

YOU'LL BE HOSTING PARTIES! You might be very excited about this, since you always throw the best parties, or you might be a bit nervous about all of the many details that go into planning a stand-out soiree in the wedding couple's honor.

To help you plan fabulous celebrations that are right on-trend and impress even if you're planning on a budget, here are some inspirations for the top types of parties that moms are now hosting during the wedding weekend.

Rehearsal Dinner

Wait, wait, wait. Isn't the rehearsal dinner the responsibility of the parents of the *groom*? Traditional etiquette has long held that the groom's side plans this party, but in today's wonderfully personalized weddings, it's entirely possible that the two families decide to switch up who will host which party—maybe they'll do the engagement party instead, since they're local to where the bride and groom live—or both sets of parents may work together on all parties. Overall, new rehearsal dinner inspirations include:

- *The wedding couple gets to use the style or theme they didn't ultimately choose for the wedding.* Let's say they originally considered a New Orleans theme for their wedding, but went with a Gatsby theme for their wedding instead. If the rehearsal dinner has a New Orleans theme, the wedding couple get one of their big wishes come true.
- *Make it a lunch instead of a dinner.* The timing might be better to get everyone together for an earlier rehearsal, and then you all go back to your place for a poolside cook-out, or to a restaurant for a lunch. An earlier party with a lighter fare menu can be far less expensive than a dinner, as well.
- *Or plan a light bites party, with a dessert bar,* if the rehearsal will be later, at 7 PM or so, because of bridal party members' arrival times.
- *Choose a private room* in a restaurant or hotel for this celebration, to keep things on the quieter side and allow toast-makers more comfort in speaking.
- *Think "farm-to-table" for the menu,* which is a big trend in catering, using farm-fresh ingredients and lighter, healthier menu options that please guests on all manner of diets.
- *Consider interactive chef stations* where guests can have their meals personalized to their wishes. This is the new wave of rehearsal dinner menus, with no one getting stuck having to choose between only two entrees included in your price fixe menu.
- *Light bites are the theme of the day* for cocktail parties, with lighter, healthier, non-greasy appetizers hand-passed and set on buffets and stations, as a replacement to the sit-down meal. Guests help themselves and mingle more this way.
- *A big trend in rehearsal dinner drink menus is flights.* A lineup of beers arranged on a platter, and paired with chef-selected foods coordinating with different beers' tastes.
- *Champagne is big,* as are champagne cocktails and menu option pairings to bubbly.
- *You can have an ornate cake for this occasion,* perhaps again in a style the wedding couple originally considered . . .

- *Or load up an indulgent desserts bar* filled with top trend sweets like macaroons, petit-fours, pastries, mini tarts, mini pies (one of the biggest dessert trends!), mason jars filled with pie makings or other desserts (also a big trend!) and vases filled with retro candies for guests to enjoy and take back to their rooms.

Not all guests have to be invited to the rehearsal dinner. We're back to just including the bridal party, their guests, and immediate family as well as the officiant and his or her partner. After this party, everyone goes to the hotel lounge to join other out-of-town guests for a cocktail gathering that you may pay for, or the wedding couple may foot the bill for. Limit the drinks to wine and beer to keep costs down.

After-Party

After the reception closes down, it's become a trend to keep the party going at one or more after-parties. By "more," this includes a separate party that you host for your friends and relatives, perhaps back at your home, while the wedding couple ventures off with their own friends on their own bar crawl. You get to unwind and reflect on the day with friends and family who have flown in for the wedding.

Here are some top trends for after-parties:

- Everyone—the wedding couple, their friends, you and your friends—goes to the hotel lounge where drinks and light bites are ordered and enjoyed. You can pick up the tab for this event (which can get pretty pricy, so think hard about your plan for this!) or everyone foots their own bills. Make sure guests know which plan you've selected for this gathering, and put details on the personal wedding website as well as in guest welcome basket itineraries.
- If you will invite your guests back to your place, you might serve from catered trays of cold foods (to make it easier on you! No slaving in the kitchen!) or set out desserts and bottles of wine and champagne.
- Nighttime pool parties are picking up steam for after-parties, so tell guests to bring their bathing suits and towels to your place.

- You might arrange for a food truck to park outside the reception site, so that guests can enjoy the fare there, or take snacks with them as they travel back home or to their hotel.
- You might also book a smaller party room in the hotel for the after-party, and plan it with a separate color scheme, table décor, new light bites menu or dessert stations, and even a deejay playing music for this late-night party.
- No favors are needed for the after-party, but it is a new trend to provide guests with late-night snacks like donuts, muffins, or "breakfast" foods to enjoy or take home.

Morning-After Breakfast

Send guests off with full bellies and perhaps something to take the edge off hang-overs with a morning-after breakfast conveniently set at the hotel.

- Guests can enjoy the hotel's inexpensive brunch, which may come with a free glass of champagne, and the brunch's elaborate spreads of food and desserts please many palates.
- Host the morning-after breakfast at your home, setting up tables outside for an al fresco party.
- Arrange for breakfast stations, so that guests can prepare their own personalized bagel topping combinations and other dishes.
- Offer a Bloody Mary bar with an array of different "heat" of sauces and celery stalk add-ins.
- Favors are a great idea at this get-together, such as baggies of frosted cookies or brownies, with a note from the couple wishing guests safe travels home.
- Don't bother arranging for pro photography or photo booths for this party, since some guests arrive tired and puffy-eyed, dressed casually and perhaps hung over from the night before. It's fine to take photos with your own camera, but the trend of having pro photos here is one that doesn't quite work and causes some wasted expense.

29

~

The Top Fifteen Do-It-Yourself Projects for Moms

MOMS ARE GETTING CRAFTY with wedding plans, often taking the lead on some of the prettiest DIY projects. Here are the top fifteen DIY projects Moms are making:

1. *Signs:* From chalkboard signs to wooden signs, hand-painted with a welcome message, the bride and groom's names, or ID-ing the food stations or dessert bar.
2. *Paper flags for food picks:* Using easy craft materials like Kraft paper and washi tape, these delicate details add pizzazz to foods, drinks and desserts.
3. *Favor labels:* In theme-matching styles, for baked items, beverages, and other gifts.
4. *Wedding programs:* Moms often design the graphics and monogram, and handle the wording for these pretty print items.
5. *Recipe book for the shower:* Collecting guests' recipes, Moms

may use Shutterfly or other online sites to create a professionally-printed book.

6   *Pie pops and desserts.*

7. *Family-favorite recipes for parties.*

8. *Garlands:* It's easy to wire up lengths of greens and accent with florals and crystals.

9. *Cake stand:* Decorated with crystals suspended from a lace-pattern cake platter edge.

10. *Paper flowers:* Small or oversized, paper flowers are a top décor trend, decorating doorways, the ceremony altar backdrop, chuppahs and trellises, and more. Here's an important note, though: paper flower templates are *copyrighted*, so take copyright law very seriously. Don't use someone else's copyrighted paper flower template to make flowers, and then sell your creations online. Know this essential rule before taking on paper flower creations.

11. *Table runners:* Take great fabric and hem the edges to add flair to table designs.

12. *Ring pillow accent:* From silk flowers to tiny butterflies, ring pillow accents are easy DIYs.

13. *Unity candles* or unity sand vessels.

14. *Mason jar etchings* or ribbon accents.

15. *Vintage luggage* decorated for guests' gift cards.

30

Mother-Daughter
Together Time

SPENDING TIME TOGETHER as mother and daughter can go a long way in de-stressing both of you. You get to enjoy and appreciate alone time with your girl, and she gets to enjoy and appreciate your calming presence and happy spirit. And even if you live many miles apart, there's always Skype to bring you closer, especially if you schedule weekly chats with each other. Making them "no wedding talk allowed" is a great idea, letting the bride escape the pressures of wedding world and getting you out of planning mind-set to just be your fun and friendly self.

Actually, making any of these get-togethers for quality Girl Time "no wedding talk allowed" events is advisable, so you can just relax, indulge, and connect.

Here are some ideas for planning quality Mother-Daughter together time:

- *A weekly TV date* to watch a sitcom, drama, or reality show together, with treats and beverages.

- *Mani/pedi appointments.* Followed by lunch or brunch at a fabulous hotel or restaurant.
- *Salad date.* If either or both of you are pre-wedding dieting, stick to your nutrition plan by going out for a salad date. You both order healthy salads with healthier dressings and indulge in good-for-you fare and great company.
- *Hiking.* Check out maps of the best places to hike in your region, according to your fitness and ability levels, and traverse together through breathtaking scenery, to waterfalls, to scenic vistas, for a half day or day of safe hiking. Adhere to all state park rule, and warning signs, and sunscreen up for your well-being.
- *Take a yoga or meditation class together.* Your yoga center might have guest passes or Groupons for a $19 month's membership so that one of you can join the other at yoga or meditation classes, or you might try out the belly dancing class or drumming circle to expand your horizons.
- *Cooking date.* Take a class at a local health food store, like Whole Foods, and learn how to prepare a healthy feast or smoothies. Or simply make a date to cook up a meal for the whole family; the two of you meet in the kitchen and spend the day prepping the meal, and invite relatives to join you for cooking tasks. After your bonding time, you both get to nurture the entire family with your creations.
- *Wine on the terrace.* Pull up a chair on the terrace, open a nice bottle of wine, and just watch the sunset, look for fireflies, or admire the gardens as you chat in this blissful, relaxing environment.
- *Go to the bookstore.* You may have taught your daughter to read, and to love reading, and now you'll continue your passion for the printed word together with regular visits to the bookstore. This may even be the start of a regular "date" you'll keep long after the wedding. You can browse the cookbooks, the newest novels, reread the classics, dig into a new series, or pick out books that you and your daughter will discuss

together, like your own little book club for two. Or four or six, if your other daughters and daughters-in-law will join in.

- *Go to a teahouse.* Teahouses are popping up all over the country, as quaint alternatives to a coffee shop, with a menu of exotic and herbal teas, scones, muffins, and other treats.
- *Go for support.* If your daughter is showing her artwork at a gallery, go to the opening and support her. If your Junior League group is having a fundraiser, invite your daughter to attend. Whatever's going on in your lives, you'll each support the other, as mother-daughter and also as friends.

31

~

Brides Tell Mother-of-the-Bride Horror Stories

Warning! Do Not Allow Yourself to Be Like These Women!

❧

My mother nixed every wedding gown I tried on. It was impossible, so I just brought her home and went back to the store alone.

—Elena, bride

❧

My mother told me I could only invite five of my twenty friends to the wedding. She just wouldn't budge. And now some of my friends aren't talking to me anymore.

—Courtney, bride

❧

My mother actually told the wedding coordinator that it was HER wedding, and I was just going to be the bride at it.

—Stephanie, bride

❧

My mother's gown cost five times as much as mine, and she received more compliments than I did at the wedding.

—Shea, bride

❧

My mother got drunk at the wedding and hit on my husband's father.

—Nancy, bride

❧

My mother got drunk at the wedding and started dancing suggestively with a twenty-five-year-old male guest. I wanted to kill her.

—Daria, bride

❧

My mother asked my husband's father for money at the reception.

—Melissa, bride

❧

My mother couldn't accept the fact that I was marrying out of my faith, so she refused to dance at the reception. She just sat all night with a sour look on her face. I was so embarrassed and hurt.

—Candace, bride

❧

My mother started screaming at my father's new wife, calling her a tramp and a home-wrecker.

—Marisol, bride

❧

My mother canceled plans I made with the wedding vendors and replaced them with her own, telling them that I gave her permission. I didn't even recognize my own wedding. When I called her on it, she said my choices were "tacky."

—Melanie, bride

My mother snuck a copy of sheet music to the organist, and told him to play her song after the one I requested. So I had to stand there at the beginning of the aisle, nervous, waiting to go to the altar, and I had to listen to a song that reminded me of another guy.

—Aimee, bride

My mother told me I should have married my ex-boyfriend.

—Lila, bride

My mother made a toast at the wedding, and she told all the guests how happy she was that I had gotten over my alcohol problem. I never had an alcohol problem. I just drank a lot in college.

—Michelle, bride

My mother told all the guests that I was pregnant at the time. We were going to wait to announce that.

—Brenda, bride

My mother told my maid of honor that I was a spoiled bitch.

—Sarah, bride

❧

My mother ruined my wedding. She was insulted that I had overruled her choice of bands, and she didn't show up on the wedding day.

—Julie, bride

❧

There's a special place of torment for mothers like these. So don't allow yourself to grow judgmental, power-hungry, vindictive, or obsessive about the wedding. You're unlikely to misbehave as these moms have, but if you don't want to wind up on Jerry Springer, keep yourself under control.

32

◡

Real Mom Stories

Looking back on their daughter's wedding days, these Moms share what they loved most, and what they'd do differently if they could go back in time:

❧

I would definitely have ASKED my daughter what she'd like me to work on, before I started making suggestions. I was just trying to help, and make the wedding extra-special, but I caused my daughter stress with what she called "meddling."

—Amy

❧

I would have kept a journal for the wedding planning time so that I could look back on all of those special little moments with my daughter and revisit my thoughts of how proud I was to help with her big day.

—Marie

My husband and I offered our daughter and her fiancé our financial contribution, without any strings attached to how they'd spend it. They had friends who battled with their parents over money, and they were profoundly grateful for the freedom to plan as they wished.

—Kelly

I would not have thrown so many "You should . . ." comments at them. Gosh, I was so annoying.

—Melanie

What an honor to join the bride in her gown shopping trips. I took a lot of "secret" photos of her during those sessions and made her a special album of those pictures.

—Justine

I wish I didn't worry so much about what other people would think about the wedding plans. My daughter is an original, and I shouldn't have lost a moment of happiness thinking family members wouldn't approve of her wishes.

—Beth

I adore my son-in-law, and was so pleased that he wanted a spotlight dance with me, in addition to his dance with his mother.

—Sara

&

I made sure I was always in a position to see my daughter's eyes during the wedding day. When she walked into her wedding ballroom, I'll never forget how happy she looked.

—Anne

&

At 5 AM on the wedding morning, I looked in on my sleeping daughter, the bride. Just like I did when she was little. What a priceless moment!

—Laura

33

Planning Mistakes to Avoid

As you work on the wedding plans, you'll want to be sure that you're operating efficiently, and that as you try to "be helpful," you're not actually stepping on the bride's toes or adding to her stress in any way. Mistakes made now live forever, after all. Clashes that happen during the wedding planning season tend to stay in the bride's memory for a long time, so keep these mistakes in mind, and don't make them!

1. *Saying "you should."* As in "You should have Cousin Anne's kids in your bridal party, since you were her flower girl 20 years ago," or "You should invite all of your second cousins to the wedding, since the family doesn't get together very often." *Shoulds* are just pressure placed on the bride. She doesn't want to upset anyone, but she doesn't want to feel obligated to expand her guest list, include kids she doesn't know in her bridal party or have wedding elements that are what you want, not what she wants. So eliminate *should* from your vocabulary, except for ultra-important things like getting insurance and checking the expiration date on her passport.

2. *Exceeding your budget.* Just like the wedding couple need to stick to their budget, so do you. If you're overspending, you could get yourself in mighty debt, cause tensions with your spouse or partner, and set a dangerous precedent for the rest of your wedding expenses. You might even overspend on your dress, leaving you with little or nothing to contribute to the wedding gift.

3. *Taking on too much DIY.* "I can do that"—"I can do that, too"—"I'll work on that" pile up on your to-do list, and when craft tasks get more complicated than you expect, and more expensive, as happens often, you might find yourself unable to complete any of the DIY tasks the bride is depending on you delivering. So keep your DIY project list on the short side, and make sure you can fulfill all of your tasks, not just the glue gun ones.

4. *Promising money before you have it.* Yes, another money one. Excited parents sometimes promise the wedding couple they'll pay for the food, the bar, the cake, the photographer, all kinds of things. When months go by, and maybe your furnace has to be replaced in your house, you're tapped out of money, and the wedding couple gets an unwelcome surprise when they find out you can't pay for what they expected you to. That's a disaster.

5. *Competing with the groom's family.* Maybe they do have more money than you do. Maybe the groom's mother wears designer clothing, and you can't afford Louboutin heels. Forget about competing with them, which never turns out well, and just do what you can, and be who you are. When you start trying to outdo the "other side," that creates tension and embarrassment for the wedding couple and also drives a wedge between you and the groom's family . . . and any battles now can wreck your relationships down the road.

6. *Being late.* The bride deals with so many people being late with their payments, size cards, and other things, and that stresses her out. So you need to be the person she knows will always deliver as promised, no

matter what it is. Return emails same-day, and deliver information and details as soon as possible.

7. *Monopolizing the wedding coordinator.* Wedding planners are happy to answer any questions you have, but if you're calling the wedding planner for every little thing, complaining to her about the plans, asking for help with diplomacy issues, and calling her every day (maybe several times a day), that's overstepping the boundaries of the relationship and stealing her time away from the bride and from her other clients. Dial it down and remember that the wedding coordinator—even if you hired her—is primarily the bride's planner.

8. *Leaving too much until the weekend of the wedding.* You may have a lot of details to attend to, but if you leave those until the last minute, you'll spend the entire wedding weekend ironing table runners and working on other tasks while everyone else is partying and mingling. So, get ahead of your to-do list and complete most of your work by a few weeks prior to the wedding. Last-minute tasks like baking cupcakes and other perishable or floral projects can be done last-minute, but not *everything.*

9. *Being disorganized.* If you can't find a receipt showing that you paid the second installment of a vendor's fee, and if you didn't record an appointment that costs you money to be a no-show for, you'll create wedding stress and chaos. Get a calendar and set up online reminders to keep yourself on track, and have *one* place to put receipts and other important documents.

10. *Not capturing your planning season memories.* Create an online folder for all of your photos, and keep a journal in which you'll record all of those wonderful little memories from this time. You'll be glad you did.

34

Troubleshooting Guide

AT MANY STEPS along the way during the planning of the wedding, problems are sure to arise. No wedding escapes without a few. Here, some mothers of brides tell you what to do when the unexpected arises.

The Planning Process

How can I be sure how much help my daughter wants?

The only way to know is to ask her. Find out in the very beginning how many jobs she wants you to do, if you'll be checking with her before you make decisions, when you'll have to hand control back to her. Give your daughter every opportunity to explain her idea of your role, and let her change her mind and change the rules as often as she needs to during the planning process.

She told me to pick whatever I want, but what if she doesn't like my decision?

If she told you to pick whatever you want, she'll have to go by your arrangements. A good rule to provide a buffer is to make sure you have a refund clause or a money-back guarantee for any contracts you arrange. If you plan far enough in advance, the companies you deal with will allow you the cancellation.

How do I get others to help us?

It takes smooth personal relations to delegate the various small jobs that the bridesmaids or the mother of the groom can handle. Just make a friendly call, and word it like this: "I wonder if you might be able to give us a hand. We really need someone to pick up some ribbon at the craft store. The order is placed, so all you have to do is pick up the order under our name. I'll give you a check." Make it easy on them, so they don't come back to you with questions and excuses that'll make you wish you just did it yourself.

My daughter is far away at school. With her time constraints, I have to book the florist and the DJ on my own. How do I make her feel included?

Send her the brochures you collect, and let her pick her idea of the top choices. When you decide, let her know which ones you picked and why, and get her final okay before you put down a deposit. The important thing is to make your daughter feel that she's not blocked out of the plans because of her faraway location.

I REALLY object to something my daughter's fiancé wants included in the ceremony. What can I do to stop it?

The bride and groom have every right to design their ceremony their own way. If it bothers you too much, speak to your daughter about it in a non-bossy way. You never know, she might hate the idea, too, and may welcome your objection. Speak rationally to the two of them. Explain why you don't like the element, and ask them to consider leaving it out as a compromise. Remember, though, that they have every right to say no. Diplomacy is everything here.

I'm not crazy about the groom or his family, and I'm very worried about their behavior during the wedding. What can I do? Do I give them an etiquette book and tell them to memorize it?

If only you could! You have to be honest about your feelings with your daughter. Tell her in a kind way—joke about it, if you can—that you don't want this to turn into a barroom brawl. She may share your concerns. You can't control the behavior of others. All you can do, if it comes down to it, is to seat his side of the

family on the opposite side of the room and stick to your side. You're the class act. So don't let them bother you. It's important to your daughter and her fiancé to have their entire families there. I'm sure they'll be on their best behavior anyway. Give them the benefit of the doubt.

My other daughter is extremely jealous of all the attention the bride is getting. She is just miserable, complaining and fighting with her sister. What can I do?

Gently tell her to grow up. Ask her to think about her sister's feelings and to put herself in her sister's shoes. How would she like it if this were the happiest time in *her* life, and someone consciously tried to take her joy away? No doubt, your other daughter feels a lot of fear and insecurity. She may feel as if she'll never get married. Assure her that her time will come, but do not be patronizing. The last thing she wants to hear is something along the lines of, "If you'd take better care of yourself/stop whining/stop smoking, you'd find a man." Yikes! Be tender with this daughter, but remind her that she only hurts other people by acting this way.

Dealing With Professionals

I'm afraid the guy I hired to take pictures will either not show up or his pictures won't come out.

It's natural to be a little nervous about the professionals you hire. After all, you don't know them and you have to take their word that they'll be everything they promised to be. But if you follow the guidelines in chapter 6, you shouldn't have any worries. Don't be concerned now about them not performing up to par. Just have a backup plan in mind in case your fears come to light, and plan to take care of business after the wedding.

What if I'm unhappy with the professionals' work during the wedding? Can I tell them to leave?

Hey, you're paying. If the photographer doesn't seem to be trying very hard to get the shots, tell him to get his act together. If he's still not performing, dismiss him. Ask a relative with a camera to cover for him and let go of all your worries. Again, you can clear away contracts after the wedding. You may have to pay the guy anyway, but at least he won't stress you out at the wedding. Sometimes a financial loss is worth the peace of mind you get by not having an unprofessional jerk around.

I'm afraid to call a lot and confirm with the vendors. They seem to be getting mad at me.

So, let them get mad at you. It's a good consumer move to confirm your orders months ahead of time, then a week ahead of time, and even the day before. True professionals will know that you're just trying to get all the details covered. Plus, many of these companies get most of their business by word of mouth. They want you to be happy with them so that you'll recommend them to your friends and family. They won't mind the extra calls.

Communication Problems

My daughter is so stressed out about everything. What can I do?

This is a stressful time for her, obviously. Beyond having to deal with the hundreds of big and little decisions that go into planning a wedding, she's about to make a major life transition. She has issues about her identity, her career, and her lifestyle that weigh heavily upon her. So give her a mental health break every so often. Go out to lunch or just for a walk, during which there is to be no talking about the wedding or any plans related to it. Give her a break and let her release some energy.

My daughter thinks I'm bossing her around. I just wanted one little thing my way.

It may seem that way to you, but your daughter is probably not getting very much her way. If she fights you because you make a request, either she's had too many requests lately or you didn't quite word it correctly. Always phrase it like this: "I hope you'll consider . . ." or "It's completely up to you, but what do you think of this. . . ." And don't fling the guilt trips. I know it may be an innate habit, but it won't do you any good here.

My daughter's bridal party members are driving her crazy. They're not following through, and they're fighting. What can I do?

You have little control over what the attendants do. But just remind your daughter that if it gets bad enough, she's better off kicking them out of the party rather than letting them ruin the entire process for her. Just don't pass notes or make secret phone calls to the irresponsible bridal party member on the bride's behalf. The bride may be offended at your actions.

Some of my family members are upset about my daughter's choices for her bridal party, and they're being rude.

So, let them be rude. If they want to pout throughout this blessed event, let them. You can't force them to grow up and remember the true meaning of family. Ignore them and tell your daughter to do the same.

One of the wedding guests penciled in the name of her date on her invitation response card. We're not allowing people to bring dates, since we're short on room. Not even the bride's sister is bringing a date. So what do I do?

Tell this horribly rude person just that. Don't worry about offending her. She obviously wasn't worried about offending you. Just say, "No dates. Sorry."

My daughter wants to invite her ex-boyfriend to the wedding. I think that's terribly unfair to the groom. What can I do?

The bride is obviously still a friend of her ex, and the groom obviously knows he's invited. If he doesn't seem to care, it only bothers you. Realize that your daughter, the groom, and the ex-boyfriend just may be mature people who can handle the fact that they've all had a past, and they can put it behind them to celebrate the present and to prepare for the future. Don't say anything at all. And don't be rude to the ex-boyfriend, even if you do remember all the pain he caused your daughter way back when. If they've struck up a friendship, that's their business.

My ex-husband plans to bring his new girlfriend to the wedding. I can't stand to see her. It will ruin my whole day.

Granted, depending on the circumstance under which your former spouse acquired this new girlfriend, it may be painful for you to see him with her. But you can do yourself and the bride no greater favor than just to pretend she isn't there. Don't sit all night glaring at them as they feed each other strawberries. Don't avoid dancing because they're dancing. You can do a solid job of just steering clear and thinking of her as just another guest while you mingle with all your loved ones—and keep your focus on your daughter and her new husband. If you are truly a gentle soul, you will realize that the new girlfriend is probably not going to be very comfortable there, as all the guests may be staring and discussing her. But she is your ex-husband's guest, and he is the father of the bride, so she does have a right to be there. Be the bigger person and let it go.

Delivery Delays

What if a delivery is late?

This is why you should keep this book handy, even on the day of the wedding. It will have your list of phone contacts so that you can call from any location to track down deliveries and give better instructions if necessary. Be sure to have a cell phone with you at the wedding.

The florist wants to charge for delivery. Can we pick up the flowers ourselves?

You can, if you wish. Just make sure you have a vehicle with plenty of room. Florist trucks keep flowers cool, so there's no wilting on the way. Think that over before you scoff at delivery charges.

Is it okay to change delivery times at the last minute?

It can't hurt to ask, but don't be surprised if it's not possible. Very often, the most popular vendors in your area will have several weddings that weekend, and they will have carefully arranged their delivery schedules to accommodate all of you. Last-minute changes may ruin those schedules, and it just may not be possible.

Ceremony Mishaps

I'm afraid I'll cry.

You may very well cry. This is an emotional time, and most parents do shed a tear or two. Just try to keep in mind that this is a joyous occasion. You can touch up your makeup afterward.

I'm afraid I'll pass out.

Just make sure you take good, deep breaths and don't lock your knees when you're standing. Stay hydrated (drink water before the ceremony), and fan yourself if you must. It's good to have something in your stomach, too. If you feel light-headed, sit down. Remember, don't panic, as that will only exacerbate your feelings of stress, and you may very well force yourself to pass out.

We're concerned that uninvited guests may try to attend the wedding. How do we stop them without creating a diversion?

If that's truly a concern, ask several family members to stand in the back of the church and keep strangers and ex-boyfriends out.

A relative's baby is notorious for crying during weddings. Can I ask her not to bring the kid to the church?

You can ask, but you risk offending your relative. A better idea might be to mention that you'll have a baby-sitter watching some of the other kids at your house during the ceremony. If that doesn't work, perhaps she'll have already tired of bringing her own child to weddings. You can always hope.

I'm afraid it will be too hot in the church.

Arrange for the officiant to have the air conditioner turned on several hours before your service. If there's no air-conditioning, ask if you can use the facility's fans or even provide your own.

What do we do about seating problems? Several relatives think they'll be in the second row.

Decide whom you want in the second row and tell the ushers to seat as such. The others will just have to purse their lips and sit in the third row. You can blame it on the ushers later. They won't mind.

Can both her father and I walk her down the aisle?

Of course! This is becoming a very common arrangement, as many brides are breaking with past traditions and honoring both their parents' wonderful jobs in raising them.

The bride has a father, and a stepfather, with whom she's really close. Who should walk her down the aisle?

That's ultimately up to the bride. If she's really torn, suggest to her that she have both of them walk her down the aisle, or that she have one walk her halfway, and the other finish the job.

The bride doesn't want anyone to walk her down the aisle. She says she's giving herself away. That's just not done.

Sure, it is. Especially with older brides, and certainly with more progressive-minded brides. If this is the bride's wish, let her have it the way she wants. Remember, she has a dream of what her wedding will be like. Let her live that dream.

Reception Dilemmas

What do we do about drunk guests?

Encourage the guest to sober up, drink coffee, or go outside for some air. Always remove the problem to a hallway or a spot far away from the bride and groom. Provide a cab ride home for a drunk guest.

What if the printed napkins and matchbooks aren't there?

Mixups like these sometimes happen. Don't let it ruin the entire party. Just tell the banquet manager you'll deal with it later. No doubt you'll get a refund, and maybe a percentage discount on the whole affair. It can't hurt to ask.

Do we keep the little problems from the bride?

You may think you're saving her from being upset about some little tiny issue. Of course, if it's nothing, then don't bother. But think about it like this. How will she feel finding out that everyone in the room knew her cake fell to the floor, and the one she cut was a fake? She may have been happier then, but the disappointment she'll feel later will last. You know the bride. Decide where you need to draw the line.

What if the food is bad?

There's little you can do once the reception is under way. That's why you should have sampled the caterer's cooking beforehand. Make a note of it.

What if the DJ plays a song that has bad memories for the family or the bride?

Talk to your DJ or band ahead of time. Give them a list of songs you really want to hear, special dances, special requests. Tell them also what you DON'T want to hear, and they should comply. If you don't do this in advance, there's not much you can do.

Transportation Problems

What if the limo doesn't show up?

Have an alternate plan and deal with the company later. Just know what you would do "in case."

What if the limo breaks down?

This has happened. Most good companies will immediately call for another car to come and transport you. If this is not an option, and you're lucky enough to have broken down at one of your locations and not on the road, load everyone into the family car and drive to the reception yourselves.

What if the driver is rude or poor with directions?

There's little *you* can do, but the bride and groom should put the driver in his place. Good research beforehand will procure an experienced driver, and you should have given the limo company good directions ahead of time. But all the planning in the world cannot prevent a driver's bad day, traffic problems, and road rage. If the driver is truly offensive, don't tip him. Report him to the limo company. You may just get a partial refund.

If Something Is Forgotten

- Send someone to go get it. Have a designated gofer who has agreed to stay sober throughout the night and be on call for quick drives and pickups.
- See if the banquet hall has any extras (they often do).
- Just forget about it and improvise.

For Major Disasters

One major disaster for any wedding is a weather event that throws a monkey wrench in all wedding plans. There may be a hurricane, snowstorm, tornado, icy roads, or some other calamity that you simply cannot do anything about. In the case of a caterer or minister not showing up, or the groom getting lost on the way to the wedding, your adrenaline will be flowing, but you can mobilize any number of helpers to make phone calls, grab your credit card and make purchases to save the day, or otherwise fly into rescue mode. No one can see these events coming, and they may in fact be your worst fears come true. The average wedding doesn't face any of these, but if you're dealt this particular hand of fate, keep the following thoughts in mind.

- Do anything you can to find a replacement.
- Call on helpful friends and family to lend a hand.
- Just shrug it off and be glad it wasn't worse.
- Remember that the important thing is that they're married.
- Try to laugh, and get the bride and groom to laugh, too.
- Try to get it on video, and you may win money on television!

35

Mother of the Bride's De-Stress Guide

FOR THOSE TIMES when the stress is unbearable, follow these calm-down rules and get yourself together.

- Just take a walk. Don't storm out of the house. Calmly go out into the fresh air and walk around the block a few times.
- Take a warm bath. A too-hot bath will cause your blood pressure to rise further.
- Try some lavender. This natural relaxer will melt your stress away. Get a dab-on perfume or light a candle.
- Herbal teas are natural calming agents. Try chamomile.
- Take a deep breath, count to eight, and let it out.
- Try progressive relaxation. Lie on a comfortable surface and relax all your muscles from head to toe.
- Listen to calming music.
- Get a massage. Here's where your husband can help you out.
- Remember to take "wedding breaks." Do not make the wedding the entire focus of your world.
- Take a fun break. Grab everyone and go to a funny movie, bowling, dancing, to the zoo, or to a park for a picnic.
- Get plenty of sleep. Your body cannot function well without it.
- Exercise produces endorphins, the body's "feel good hormone." So pull that unused exercise equipment out of the basement and embark on a safe exercise regimen.

36

Resources for
All Your Wedding Needs

Wedding-Related Websites

THIS LIST IS PURELY FOR YOUR RESEARCH USE, and does not imply endorsement or recommendation of the companies or products. Since websites and apps may change over time, we apologize if any Web addresses have changed since the time of this printing.

Mother of the Bride Dresses

Beautiful Mothers by Mary's:
   MarysBridal.com
Cameron Blake:
   CameronBlake.com
Capri by Mon Cheri:
   CapribyMonCheri.com
Caterina: JordanFashions.com

Collection 20: Watters.com
David's Bridal: DavidsBridal.com
House of Brides:
   HouseofBrides.com
Intermezzo by Venus:
   VenusBridals.com
Ivonne D.:
   MontagebyMonCheri.com
Jade: JasmineBridal.com

Jasmine Black Label:
   JasmineBridal.com
Jovani: Jovani.com
Landa: LandaDesigns.com
Love by Enzoani: Enzoani.com
Montage by Mon Cheri:
   MontagebyMonCheri.com
Olga Kvitko Couture:
   OlgaKvitko.com
Saison Blanche Social Occasion:
   SaisonBlanche.com
Siri: SiriInc.com
Social Occasions by Mon Cheri:
   SocialOccasionsbyMonCheri.com
Ursula: Ursula.com
Val Stefani C2: ValStefani.com
Val Stefani Celebrations:
   ValStefani.com
Venus: Venus.com
VM by Mori Lee: MoriLee.com

Department Stores and Clothing Stores

AnnTaylor.com
Belk.com
Bloomingdales.com
JCrew.com
Macys.com
Nordstrom.com
WhiteHouseBlackMarket.com

Dress Trade

BridesmaidTrade.com
NewlyMaid.com

Shoes and Accessories

AllureBridals.com
AnnaSeth.com
AnnTaylor.com
BeverlyFeldmanShoes.com
BHLDN.com
BridalShoes.com
ChineseLaundry.com
ChristianLouboutin.com
DavidsBridal.com
Dessy.com
DiscountWeddingShoes.com
DSW.com
JasonWuStudio.com
JCPenney.com
KateSpade.com
MyGlassSlipper.com
MyLittlePretty.com
NeimanMarcus.com
NinaShoes.com
ShoeBuy.com
Shoes.com
StuartWeitzman.com
Zappos.com

Beauty

Avon.com

BobbiBrown.com

CareFair.com

Clinique.com

ElizabethArden.com

EsteeLauder.com

Eve.com

iBeauty.com

Lancome.com

L'oreal.com

MacCosmetics.com

MakeoverStudio.com

MaxFactor.com

Maybelline.com

Neutrogena.com

Pantene.com

Revlon.com

Sephora.com

HairStyles

About.com

Beauty-and-the-Bath.com

DIY-Weddings.com

eHow.com

HairstyleZone.com

HerbalEssences.com

Suave.com

UpDoPrincess.com

VideoHairstyles.com

YouTube.com

Wedding Planning Websites

100LayerCake.com

BridalGuide.com

Brides.com

DestinationIDoMag.com

GetMarried.com

GreenWeddingShoes.com

Idoforbrides.com

MarthaStewart.com

MunaluchiBride.com

PolkaDotBride.com

StyleMePretty.com

SouthernBride.com

TheKnot.com

TownandCountry.com

WeddingChannel.com

WellWed.com

Invitations

AnnaGriffin.com

BotanicalPaperworks.com

CeciNewYork.com

Crane.com

Evite.com

Hallmark.com

InviteSite.com

MomentalDesigns.com

MountainCow.com

PaperStyle.com

Papyrus.com

Preciouscollection.com

PSAEssentials.com
WeddingPaperDivas.com

Quotes and Poetry

QuoteGarden.com
QuotesandSayings.org
QuotesPlanet.com
@TheLoveStories

Music and Lyrics

iTunes.com
LyricsDepot.com
LyricsFreak.com
Romantic-Lyrics.com
Spotify.com

Flowers and Greenery

BHG.com
HGTV.com
PAllenSmith.com
About.com
FloralDesignInstitute.com
RomanticFlowers.com
SierraFlowerFinder.com

Food and Recipes

AllRecipes.com
BHG.com
CookingLight.com
FoodNetwork.com

Wine and Champagne

FoodandWine.com
Wine.com
WineSpectator.com

Crafts and Paper

BHG.com
FlaxArt.com
HobbyLobby.com
MarthaStewart.com
Michaels.com
OfficeMax.com
PaperDirect.com
Scrapjazz.com
Staples.com

Travel

Bed and Breakfast Finder:
   www.bnbfinder.com
Tourism Office Worldwide Directory:
   TOWD.com

Price Comparison Sites

BizRate.com
Dealtime.com
NextTag.com
PriceGrabber.com
Shopping.com
Shopzilla.com
@AboutFreebies

Coupon Sources

AllYou.com
CouponCabin.com
CouponDivas.com
CouponMom.com
Coupons.com
Groupon.com
LivingSocial.com
RetailMeNot.com
SwagGrabber.com

Bartering Sites

(Use wisely, with safety in mind, and read the fine print on the site and swaps.)
Badabud.com
BarterPlanet.com
BarterQuest.com
PeopleTradingServices.com

Skills2Barter.com
SwagAGift.com
SwapStyle.com
SwapTree.com
ThingHeap.com
Trashbank.com
U-Exchange.com

Bridal Expos

BridalShowcase.com
BridalShowExpo.com
Brideworld.com
ElegantBridalProductions.com
GreatBridalExpo.com
HereComestheGuide.com
TheBlingEvent.com
TheWeddingSalon.com
WeddingWire.com/bridalshows

Additional Sites of Interest

WeddingMapper *Create your own wedding map, share the URL, and use their seating tool and budget tracker for free.*
WilliamsSonoma.com Free cooking classes and events.

Free Wedding Apps

Just some of the free apps in the Apple iTunes store, helping brides, moms, and 'maids with wedding planning tasks.
SnapKnot *Help with photography.*
WedPics *Organize your wedding photos from all of the wedding celebrations.*

Lover.ly *Gorgeous images to inspire you.*

All Seated *Help with creating seating plans.*

Wedding Happy *An overall wedding planning help site organizing your to-do's and showing you the percentage of your planning that's done.*

Wedding Countdown *A fun tool showing you how many days left until the wedding.*

iDoo *Complete wedding planning task organizer.*

Martha Stewart Weddings Magazine *Yes, for free.*

iWedding *Planning organizer and interactive tools.*

Wilton Cake Ideas and More *If you'll DIY cakes and desserts or are just tasked with getting a cake for a celebration, this app helps you with designs.*

Visit iTunes.com for more free apps to help you out. . . .

Worksheets

Phone Call Records

Date	Time	Spoke To	About

Confirmation Worksheet

Category	Spoke To	1st Confirm Date	2nd Confirm Date	Noted
Wedding dress salon				
Bridesmaids' dresses				
Shoes				
Florist				
Caterer				
Limo company				
Photographer				
Videographer				
DJ/Band				
Officiant				
Wedding cake				
Tuxedos				
Your wardrobe				

Category	Spoke To	1st Confirm Date	2nd Confirm Date	Noted
Honeymoon flight				
Honeymoon reservations				
Hotel rooms				
Shuttle service				
Ceremony musicians				

Contact List

Wedding couple cell phone _____

Wedding couple e-mail _____

Wedding coordinator _____

Floral designer _____

Maid of honor _____

Bridesmaids _____

_____

_____

Flower girl parents _____

Stationer or printer _____

Caterer _____

Baker _____

Favors _____

Hotel manager _____

Hotel concierge _____

Transportation _____

Gown shop _____

Alterations _____

Others _____

_____

DIY Project Worksheet

Project name _____

Who will work on

  this with you _____

_____

_____

Supplies needed

_____

_____

_____

_____

Budget _____

Deadline for

  completion _____

Date to show 1st

  progress report _____

Where to deliver _____

Special instructions _____

_____

_____

_____

(Copy this form for each of your DIY projects.)

Delegation List

_____

_____

_____

_____

_____

_____

_____

_____

_____

_____

_____

_____

_____

_____

_____

_____

_____

_____

_____

_____

_____

_____

_____

_____

Shopping List

Rentals Needed

For which event? _____

Date of event _____

Rental shop

   contact info _____

Order date _____

Delivery date _____

Items needed _____

_____

_____

_____

_____

_____

_____

_____

_____

_____

Return date and

   time: _____

(Copy this form for each event involving rentals.)

Author's Closing Notes

THERE WILL BE a million details, a million little problems, a million joys and memories. Planning a wedding is one of the largest undertakings you may experience in your life, and it's a big job that will be worth every moment of worrying, hassling, and hoping.

In the end, what matters is that your daughter is married to her true love. You've helped her put together the wedding of her dreams, and these memories will last a lifetime for both of you.

I hope you'll always remember to enjoy the process. Savor the moments. Be proud that you were able to give your daughter the wedding of her dreams. So many parents, for some reason or another, simply cannot. And you have been graced with the honor and ability to give your child what so many parents only wish they could.

Make the day one of pure joy and celebration of love.

You're going to be wonderful, Mom.

☙

At all times, ask, "Is this what the bride wants?"

—Shea, bride

☙

The best you can do is all you can do. So just hope for the best always, and make everything into a positive.

—Joanne, mother of the bride

Index

About the Author

SHARON NAYLOR is the author of over 35 wedding books and an acclaimed expert on the subject of tying the knot in style. She has served as the iVillage wedding expert and blogger, host of *Here Come the Moms* on Wedding Podcast Network, the *Bridal Guide* budget expert with a new e-mail-a-day feature, wedding advice guru at Weddzilla.com, consultant to Bed Bath & Beyond, contributing editor to *Southern Bride,* and contributor to numerous bridal magazines. She has been a frequent guest on *Martha Stewart Weddings* on Sirius Satellite Radio and on TV shows including *Good Morning America, ABC News, Get Married, I Do! with The Knot,* and *Lifetime.* She has been featured in *InStyle Weddings, Modern Bride, Brides, Bridal Guide, Hallmark, Redbook, Martha Stewart Weddings, The Wall Street Journal, Glamour, Marie Claire,* and many other publications. She lives in the New York City area. For more information, visit her at www.sharonnaylor.net.